THE

RE-JUSTIFICATION

OF GOD

AN EXEGETICAL & THEOLOGICAL STUDY OF ROMANS 9:10-24

THE

RE-JUSTIFICATION

OF GOD

AN EXEGETICAL & THEOLOGICAL STUDY OF ROMANS 9:10-24

J. D. MYERS

RedeemingPress.com

THE RE-JUSTIFICATION OF GOD:
An Exegetical and Theological Study of Romans 9:10-24
© 2017 by J. D. Myers

Published by Redeeming Press
Dallas, OR 97338
RedeemingPress.com

ISBN: 978-1-939992-49-9 (Paperback)
ISBN: 978-1-939992-40-6 (Mobi)
ISBN: 978-1-939992-41-3 (ePub)

JOIN JEREMY MYERS AND LEARN MORE

Take Bible and theology courses by joining Jeremy at
RedeemingGod.com/join/

Receive updates about free books, discounted books,
and new books by joining Jeremy at
RedeemingGod.com/reader-group/

TAKE THE
RE-JUSTIFICATION OF GOD
ONLINE COURSE

Join others at RedeemingGod.com/join/
to take the online course and discuss this book with others

Thanks for reading!

Other Books by Jeremy Myers

Nothing but the Blood of Jesus
The Atonement of God
What is Prayer?
Adventures in Fishing (for Men)
*Christmas Redemption: Why Christians Should Celebrate a
    Pagan Holiday*
Why You Have Not Committed the Unforgivable Sin
The Gospel According to Scripture
The Gospel Dictionary

Books in the "Close Your Church for Good" Series

Introduction: Skeleton Church
Volume 1: The Death and Resurrection of the Church
Volume 2: Put Service Back into the Church Service
Volume 3: Church is More than Bodies, Bucks, & Bricks
Volume 4: Dying to Religion and Empire
Volume 5: Cruciform Pastoral Leadership

All books are available at Amazon.com
Learn about each title at the end of this book

For all Calvinists.
You have made me think and re-think what I truly believe.

TABLE OF CONTENTS

FOREWORD

Have you ever agonized over election and predestination? I certainly have. Soon after believing in Jesus at seventeen, I got involved in the debates between Calvinists and Arminians over passages like Romans 9. I had no idea what to make of them. And it tore me up.

Was I Jacob or Esau?

Did God love me or hate me?

How could I know for sure?

As I think back to those times, I realize I was exposed to a limited number of viewpoints, largely biased towards Calvinism. That's all I heard. As I result, I became a reluctant Calvinist and, quite frankly, it robbed me of my Christian joy. How couldn't God love everyone? Does that mean God might not love me?

If someone had given me a book like J. D. Myers' *The Re-Justification of God*, it would have saved me so much heartache. I believe it will fundamentally change how you read Romans and how you understand election.

In particular, Myers makes a very convincing case for two big ideas.

The first big idea concerns salvation. Do you think you know what it means in Romans? Have you ever considered that salvation means more than forensic justification? Have you considered that, in Romans, you are "saved" after you are justified? Did you know that salvation is something that born-again believers experience? That opens up so many different possibilities.

The second big idea concerns election. Have you ever considered that election can be to service, not to eternal life? That's what Myers argues. Despite popular opinion to the contrary, Romans 9 is not about God's choosing this or that individual to have eternal life. Rather, it is about God's choosing this or that group to serve His purposes.

In particular, Romans 9 answers the question—is God through with Israel? Will He no longer use her? Has He abandoned the promises made to her?

Not at all.

As Myers explains Paul's argument,

> God wants to bless the world through His people, and if one group of people fails in this God-given task, then God will simply find someone else to do it while He continues to lead the first group to fulfill His overarching purposes—albeit in different ways than originally intended."

Myers keeps bringing us back to the basic truth that election is to service and it is amazing to see how much light that shines on Romans 9.

Despite the topic, anyone can read this book.

Myers makes his case in a very understandable way.

So if you are a serious Bible student, you should read this book.

I'm sure you will find it convincing. I certainly did.

At the very least, reading it will broaden your horizons. You'll see there are more options on the table than what you will typically hear from Calvinist or Arminian writers. And that in itself will repay you dividends. You'll learn to be a more careful interpreter of God's Word. And you might come away with a greater assurance that you, too, are chosen to serve Him.

Shawn Lazar
Author of *Chosen to Serve: Why Divine Election Is to Service, Not to Eternal Life*

November 2017
Denton, TX

AUTHOR'S NOTE

As you read through this brief study, there will be numerous places where you will wish for more footnotes, references, and citations. Please note that a lack of citations does not indicate a lack of research. As I will explain in the Preface below, this book is an initial draft of a much longer and more detailed book I wish to write someday. I have been studying Romans 9 for most of my adult life in one way or another, so that much of what is written on these pages is little more than a summation of the theological thought and exegetical research that I have undertaken in recent decades. Whether this book shows it or not, much of the hard exegetical work on Romans 9 has been done. This short book contains only the first fruits of my labor, even if it doesn't show how I plowed the field, planted the seed, watered the soil, pulled the weeds, and cultivated the plants.

Take the words "salvation" and "wrath" as examples. These are two of the key terms in Romans. Most students of Romans assume that they know what Paul means by these words. They believe that salvation refers to justification, the forgiveness of sins, and the reception of eternal life so that a person can go to heaven when they die. Likewise, people assume that wrath is the opposite of this, and refers to everlasting punishment in hell. These definitions of these key terms then guide how the student of Paul's letter to the Romans understands what Paul is teaching. Very early in the study below, I will propose alternative definitions for these two terms. I will not, however, go into great detail defending these alternative definitions. But do not mistake the lack of exegetical evidence or footnotes as a sign that no hard work has been done. The work has been done; it simply doesn't make an appearance here. I explain why in the Preface.

So as you read along, if you find yourself thinking, "Where's the exegesis?" know (1) that it does exist, and (2) maybe the challenging idea you just read is an invitation for you to engage in your own exegetical work "to see if these things are so."

PREFACE

Nearly two decades ago when, as a Five-Point Calvinist, I began to question whether or not Calvinism truly reflected the biblical gospel, someone invited me to read John Piper's book *The Justification of God: An Exegetical and Theological Study of Romans 9:1-23.* I was told that this book would settle the matter once and for all, that I would be convinced as never before about the truth of Calvinism, and especially the Calvinistic doctrine of Unconditional Election.

So I bought the book and read it.

Ironically, far from convincing me of the truth of Calvinism, it was Piper's book more than any other which caused me to see that there were serious problems with how Calvinists read, understood, and applied Scripture. In his book, John Piper set out to clear God's name of any wrongdoing in regards to the oft-misunderstood doctrine of election. By taking a careful look at Romans 9:1-23 Piper wanted to show how the Apostle Paul defended the righteousness of God in connection to the doctrine of election.

Why does the righteousness of God need defending? Many feel that it is unjust or unfair for God to decide, in eternity past, whom to bless with eternal life, and whom to condemn with eternal damnation. It seems unjust that God should decide the eternal destiny of all people from eternity past, without any consideration whatsoever about their desires in the matter, or their actions for good or evil. So in *The Justification of God,* Piper set out to show how Paul defended the right of God to do exactly as He did in regards to people's eternal destinies.

As I read Piper's book, I became more and more concerned. It seemed to me that, far from justifying the actions of God, Piper was making God *more* monstrous and immoral than I had ever imagined. By the end of the book, I had become convinced that Piper had completely failed in *The Justification of God* to justify God at all, but had instead accomplished the condemnation of God. In an attempt to defend God from the accusations of pagans about there being injustice with God, Piper had simply made God into a pagan deity who more closely resembled the three Fates of Greek Mythology than the incarnation of God in Jesus Christ.

I decided then and there that what was needed was a response to Piper's book titled *The Re-Justification of God.* I wanted to provide an exegetically-based and theologically-sound explanation of Romans 9. But, as I was still (mostly) a Calvinist, I knew I was nowhere near ready to write this book. I had to study and read, and study and read. So I set out to do just this. What followed was a twenty-year (and counting) journey out of Calvinism.

Now, nearly twenty years later, I have written a book with the title I had originally imagined, and the book cover as well. Did you notice that the cover to this book is incredibly boring? This is because it is a near replica of the book by John Piper, but I used an "editorial" mark to add the prefix "Re-" to Justification. So rather than *The Justification of* God, we now have *The Re-Justification of God.* So the cover is boring on purpose. This had been planned from the very beginning.

However, despite the book cover being exactly as I wanted (as boring as it is), the book content is not the book I originally intended to write. This book is not a point-by-point refutation of John Piper's book. Though the content of this book is similar to what I wanted to write in the book I had imagined, this one is little more than an outline (or maybe a preview or a foretaste) of the book I wanted to write. This book is half-baked. (I included that line just so my Calvinist friends could accuse me of writing this book while I was "half-baked.") This book contains the basic approach and theology that I believe Paul is teaching in Romans 9, but contains very little of the all-important exegetical argumentation that is required to defend it. Some exegesis is included; but not nearly all. That is why this book is not the book I originally intended to write. This book is not finished. It's not even half-way done.

So why even publish it? Why didn't I just take another year or two and complete the book? Why put out a book which contains the theology I believe Paul is teaching in Romans 9 without also including the critical exegetical evidence needed to support that theology? In doing so, am I not setting myself up for failure? For criticism? For condemnation? For attack?

Yes, I am.

But the reason I am putting this book out before it is done is because this book is a rabbit trail of a rabbit trail of a rabbit trail of a rabbit trail. Let me explain.

Three years ago I set out to write a commentary on the book of Jonah. I wrote about 50,000 words on the first chapter of Jonah, but soon realized I had some difficulties with the theology of Jonah, specifically with the idea that God sends storms upon people. So I embarked on my first rabbit trail. I set out to study what the Bible taught about the violence of God.

My study of the violence of God went well for a year or two. I learn by writing, so I wrote about 100,000 words on the theology of a violent God and how we can understand God in light of the revelation we have received in Jesus Christ. This study progressed well until I began to do the hard work of exegesis. I soon discovered that the way I read Scripture would not support the theology I was trying to defend. So I faced a dilemma. I could change my theology of God to match the way I read Scripture, or I could reconsider the way I read Scripture. Since I believe that Jesus is the ultimate revelation of God, I went with the second option, and decided to rethink how I read Scripture. I sought to read Scripture through the lens of Jesus, rather than re-interpret Jesus in light of the way I read Scripture. By viewing the Scriptures through Jesus, I realized that my problem with the violence of God in the Bible was really a problem with how I read the Bible itself.

So I set out on my second rabbit trail of trying to rethink everything I have ever thought about Scripture. I began to ask questions about the Bible. Questions like, What kind of Bible do we have? Are we reading the Bible the way it was intended to be read, or are we reading the Bible in the way we want it to behave? I wanted to rediscover the Bible *as it is*, rather than read the Bible *as I wanted it*. I wrote about another 50,000 words on this second rabbit trail as I tried to rethink my Bibliology.

It dawned on me one day, however, that the problem wasn't so much with my Bibliology, but with my Theology Proper itself. Reading the Bible the way I wanted it rather than the way it truly is had a foundation in worshipping God as I want Him rather than the way He truly is. Since my theology has its foundation in the Reformation, I started chasing after this third rabbit by writing about Calvinism. In Bible College I had adopted a Calvinistic approach to God and Scripture, but over the last two decades or so, I began to see that this approach may not be correct. So I set out to re-study Calvinism within the light of Scripture. I got about 100,000 words into this third rabbit trail before I bumped into Romans 9.

My study of Romans 9 became the fourth rabbit trail from my study of Jonah. I was starting to panic. I really, *really* wanted to get back to Jonah and was starting to despair that this would ever happen. I was over three years and 250,000 words away from it, with no end in sight. I knew that Romans 9 was a lynchpin in Reformed theology, and I knew I had to deal with it in order to finish my study of the Calvinistic God, which in turn was needed to help me understand the God who gave us the Bible, which in turn was needed to understand the Bible itself, which in turn was needed to understand the violent portions of the Bible, which in turn was needed to understand the book of Jonah. I also knew that writing a full book on Romans 9 which included all of my exegetical research on the passage would take about a year to write and another 50,000 words or so. Maybe more. So I decided to shelve the full-length book and just write a summary of what I believe Paul is teaching in Romans 9. That summary is this short book. Will I ever get around to writing the full-length book I wanted to write, which includes all the necessary exegetical evidence needed to support my reading of Romans 9? I do not know. Let me get back to Jonah first, and then we'll go from there.

This short book on Romans 9:10-24 will have to do for now. It contains an alternative to the Calvinistic way of reading Romans 9 which has been popular in some circles for hundreds of years. And though I do not include most of the exegetical details needed to fully defend the approach presented here, this does not mean the hard work of exegesis was not done. I simply chose, in the interest of time, to leave most of the exegesis out. I will include it in a future expanded edition (if I ever get to it). As a result of leaving most of the exegesis out, I fully know that most Calvinists will not be persuaded by my approach. Most Calvinists are quite intelligent and detail-oriented, needing sound exegetical evidence for any challenge to their theology. I say this to their praise. May more Christians adopt this trait! So this book is not intended to persuade them. Instead, this book is intended to do a few other things.

First, this book is for people who are not Calvinists but who are researching Calvinism. Since there is a glut of books on the Christian market which teach and defend the Calvinistic approach to Scripture, I hope this book can show people that there is another way of reading Scripture and understanding God. Again, considering the lack of exegesis in this book, maybe these people won't be convinced either. But at least they will be introduced to the idea that there is another way, and maybe they will embark on an exegetical study of their own.

Second, this book is intended to let Calvinists know that there are perspectives on Scripture other than Calvinism and Arminianism. I am not an Arminian. When it comes to studies on Romans 9, I heartily agree with most Calvinists that the Arminian explanation of this text is quite weak. This is generally true of many aspects of Arminian theology. But when I read Calvinistic books, or Arminian for that matter, it seems that neither group is aware of any sort of mediating position between the two polar extremes. Both Calvinists and Arminians seem to be ignorant of anybody but Calvinists and Arminians. This then leads the average person in the pew with the feeling that when it comes to the debate between Calvinism and Arminianism, they must choose between the two. This book, hopefully, will allow people to see that there are other viable perspectives! This book presents one of them, albeit in a perfunctory and condensed fashion.

Thirdly and finally, I simply want this book to be another voice in the ongoing discussion about Romans 9. Clearly, I do not have the final word. I have already stated multiple times that this book is not complete. Even if it were, this book would still not be the final word on Romans 9. Christians will always debate this text until Jesus returns. Maybe even after … (One thing I plan to do in heaven is sit down with Paul and ask him if, in light of all the debate about this chapter, he would still write Romans 9 the way he did. If the Apostle Paul is reading this—as a member of the great cloud of witnesses—please mark me down for an appointment.) Here's the point: I am putting this theology of Romans 9 out there now so that people can interact with it and consider a different perspective on Romans 9. I hope to hear what people say about this approach so that I can modify or better explain this perspective in future editions of this work.

With all this in mind, let the conversation begin ...

INTRODUCTION

When it comes to the discussion of divine election, almost all Calvinists always refer to Romans 9. It is the premier election passage, bar none. Edwin Palmer says that Romans 9 contains the "finest statement of all" about election.[1] James Montgomery Boice and Philip Graham Ryken call it "the most important passage."[2] While all of Romans 9–11 is frequently pointed to as evidence for the doctrine of Unconditional Election by God of individuals to eternal life, the text that often gets the most attention is Romans 9:10-24:

> *And not only this, but when Rebecca also had conceived by one man, even by our father Isaac (for the children not yet being born, nor having done any good or evil, that the purpose of God according to election might stand, not of works but of Him who calls), it was said to her, "The older shall serve the younger." As it is written, "Jacob I have loved, but Esau I have hated."*

[1] Edwin H. Palmer, *The Five Points of Calvinism*, Enl. ed. (Grand Rapids: Baker, 1980), 32.

[2] James Montgomery Boice and Philip Graham Ryken, *The Doctrines of Grace: Rediscovering the Evangelical Gospel* (Wheaton: Crossway, 2002), 92.

What shall we say then? Is there unrighteousness with God? Certainly not! For He says to Moses, "I will have mercy on whomever I will have mercy, and I will have compassion on whomever I will have compassion."

So then it is not of him who wills, nor of him who runs, but of God who shows mercy. For the Scripture says to Pharaoh, "For this very purpose I have raised you up, that I may show My power in you, and that My name may be declared in all the earth." Therefore He has mercy on whom He wills, and whom He wills He hardens.

You will say to me then, "Why does He still find fault? For who has resisted His will?" But indeed, O man, who are you to reply against God? Will the thing formed say to him who formed it, "Why have you made me like this?" Does not the potter have power over the clay, from the same lump to make one vessel for honor and another for dishonor?

What if God, wanting to show His wrath and to make His power known, endured with much longsuffering the vessels of wrath prepared for destruction, and that He might make known the riches of His glory on the vessels of mercy, which He had prepared beforehand for glory, even us whom He called, not of the Jews only, but also of the Gentiles? (Rom 9:10-24)

Though Calvinists claim that Romans 9:10-24 is one of the central texts for their doctrine of Unconditional Election, this passage is actually one of the clearest New Testament texts which defends the truth that election is to service and purpose rather than to eternal life. Before we see how this is so, let us allow several Calvinists to weigh in on Romans 9. Though there are many extended treatments of Romans 9 by Calvinists which are too long to quote here,[3] the following quotes succinctly summarize what the majority of Calvinists believe regarding this passage.

> Throughout Romans 9–11 Paul assumes that election deals with individuals and with eternal destinies, and that it is unconditional. There is, I believe, a divine covenantal commitment to corporate Israel, but that does not contradict or annul the individual, eternal thrust of Romans 9. The principle of unconditionality is seen most clearly in Romans 9:11. God elects this way so that "though they were not yet born and had done nothing either good or bad, in order that God's purpose of election might continue."[4]

> This passage gives strong exegetical support to a traditional Calvinistic interpretation of God's election: God chooses those who will be saved on the basis of his own will and not on the basis of anything—works or faith, whether seen or not—in those human beings so chosen.[5]

> ... in Romans 9 ... Paul has demonstrated conclusively that salvation is not of him that works but of him that calls, and that election is unconditional. ... Salvation does not depend on the man who

---

[3] See, for example, John Piper, *The Justification of God: An Exegetical and Theological Study of Romans 9:1-23* (Grand Rapids: Baker, 1983); A. W. Pink, *The Sovereignty of God* (Grand Rapids: Baker, 1930), 85-98.

[4] John Piper, *Five Points: Toward a Deeper Understanding of God's Grace* (Geanies House, Scotland: Christian Focus, 2014), 56. For a detailed explanation of this passage from a Calvinistic perspective, see Piper, *The Justification of God*

[5] Douglas J. Moo, *The Epistle to the Romans*, ed. F.F. Bruce Ned B. Stonehouse, & Gordon D. Fee, The New International Commentary on the New Testament (Grand Rapids: Eerdmans, 1996), 587.

wills, wants, or decides; nor on him who runs. It depends solely on
God who has mercy.[6]

If the words of inspired Scripture in Romans 9 do not speak with
sufficient clarity to the topic, what could? ... When the passage is
allowed to speak for itself, it speaks of unconditional election in the
plainest terms. It is God's mercy, not man's will or effort, that de-
termines the outcome of salvation.[7]

The presence of a strong concept of predestination cannot be de-
nied, although only here does Paul present double-predestination.
Not until this is admitted without reserve can one see its necessary
delimitations and ask about its significance within the framework of
the apostle's theology. ... Since the theme is Israel, the issue is sote-
riology. From v. 12a it follows even more precisely that the doctrine
of the justification of the ungodly is anchored in the sovereign freedom of the Creator. ... God's word comes on the scene as a stigma-
tizing address with which salvation or perdition takes place for human beings.[8]

This last quote by Ernst Käsemann is highly revealing. Not
only does he state that this passage cannot be understood *unless*
we see that Paul is teaching double predestination, he then goes
on to reveal his confusion about the text by equating salvation
with justification. Even more interesting is that when Käsemann

---

[6] Palmer, *Five Points*, 34.

[7] Dave Hunt and James White, *Debating Calvinism: Five Points, Two Views*
(Sisters, OR: Multnomah, 2004), 98.

[8] Ernst Käsemann and Geoffrey William Bromiley, *Commentary on Romans*
(Grand Rapids: Eerdmans, 1980), 265-266. Note that Ernst Käsemann is Lutheran, but his words represent the view of many Calvinists.

first begins to deal with Romans 9–11, he writes that "no part of this epistle is so self-contained [and] none may be detached so easily or, as it seems, at so little risk."[9] In other words, he doesn't see exactly how Romans 9–11 fits within Paul's epistle to the Romans as a whole, and indeed, even says that these chapters could be removed from Paul's letter without much risk to Paul's overall message and theme. The only way Käsemann is able to keep his understanding of Romans 9–11 attached to the rest of Paul's epistle is by saying that "the schemata of the doctrine of justification are forcibly introduced into the context."[10] In other words, according to Käsemann, Romans 9–11 do not seem to fit Paul's overall argument, and so the doctrine of justification must be unnaturally forced into them so that they do fit.

I wonder if it might be better to understand that Paul's letter to the Romans is not primarily about justification after all, and in this way, see that Romans 9–11 naturally follows (indeed, is *forced* by) Paul's message in Romans 1–8. When we properly understand Romans, we cannot agree with Käsemann that Romans 9–11 could easily be detached from Paul's letter with little risk to Paul's message. When we properly understand Romans, we see that far from being an easily-discarded afterthought or culturally-bound and theologically-arcane rabbit trail, Romans 9–11 is the pinnacle of Paul message, forming the necessary hinge between what Paul has written in Romans 1–8 to how Paul applies this message in Romans 12–15. Without Romans 9–11, Romans 1–8

[9] Ibid., 253.
[10] Ibid., 264.

would be little more than an interesting theological inquiry, and without Romans 9–11, Paul could not have written Romans 12–15. When taken as a whole, we see that Paul's letter to the Romans is not about justification, or even the righteousness of God. Paul's letter to the Romans is about how the gospel "saves" believers and unbelievers alike (Rom 1:16-17). This becomes clearer when we recognize that the word "saves" does not mean "justifies" but "delivers." Paul's letter to the Romans is about how the gospel not only delivers people from the eternal and spiritual consequences of sin, but also from the temporal and physical consequences. Romans 9–11 fits squarely within the second part of this theme.

Up to this point in Romans, Paul has been saying that God has a divine purpose and significance for all believers, and if they will live in light of their justification (Romans 4–5) and walk by faith (Romans 6–7), then God will bless them and work with them to accomplish His will on earth (Romans 8). In the last part of Romans 8, Paul sets out to encourage his readers that nothing can get in God's way of accomplishing His purposes. The obvious objection to this idea, of course, concerns Israel. Israel too was God's elect. Israel too was God's chosen people. But by all appearances, God "set them aside" and turned to the Gentiles instead. The objection to the point Paul makes in Romans 8 is, "But God's purposes failed with Israel, didn't they? How can we know His purposes for us won't fail as well?" In Romans 9–11, Paul explains why God's purposes did not fail, and that God has not set Israel aside, but that what happened to Israel is nevertheless something that can happen to Gentile Christians as well.

A complete explanation of how Paul develops these themes in

his letter requires a full-length commentary on Romans. For now, let us simply focus on several keys that help us understand what Paul is saying in Romans 9:10-24 (and Romans 9–11) in light of the overall context of Romans. Before we can examine the text of Romans 9:10-24, we must understand three contextual keys to this section of Romans. We must understand what Paul means by the word "salvation," that election is to service, and that election can be both individual and corporate. Let us look at these three contextual keys.

CHAPTER 1

SALVATION IN ROMANS

To begin with, we must recognize that "salvation" in Scripture rarely refers to receiving eternal life. "Salvation" does not mean "forgiveness of sins so we can go to heaven when we die." The word simply means "deliverance," and the context must determine what sort of deliverance is in view. Most often, the deliverance is some sort of physical deliverance from enemies, storms, and sickness, or from some of the temporal consequences of sin (cf. Matt 8:25; 9:22; Mark 5:34; 13:20; Luke 8:48; 23:35; John 12:27; 1 Tim 2:15; 2 Tim 4:18; Jas 5:15; Jude 5).[1] This understanding of "salvation" is especially true in Romans.

Most of the uses of "salvation" in Romans are in connection with wrath. It is not wrong to say that "salvation in Romans" is deliverance from wrath.[2] So what is wrath? Just as salvation does not refer to entrance into heaven, wrath does not refer to eternity in hell. Nor is wrath from God. Though an imaginary objector to

---

[1] See "save, saving" in W. E. Vine, Merrill F. Unger, and William White Jr., *Vine's Complete Expository Dictionary of Old and New Testament Words* (Nashville: Thomas Nelson, 1985).

[2] Zane C. Hodges, *Romans: Deliverance from Wrath* (Corinth, TX: GES, 2013).

Paul does occasionally speak of "God's wrath" in Romans, Paul does not understand wrath this way. For Paul, "wrath" is what happens to people (both believers and unbelievers) when they stray from God's guidelines for proper living. Today, we would speak of "consequences." While someone today might say that a destroyed marriage is the consequence of adultery, Paul might argue that a destroyed marriage is the "wrath" of adultery. And as all who have experienced the damaging and destructive consequences of sin know, the fall-out from sinful choices often feels like wrath. Sin brings metaphorical earthquakes, hailstorms, raging fires, and flash floods into our lives, leaving behind large swaths of destruction. What better word to describe this than "wrath"?

Even still, this "wrath" is not "from" God any more than a ruined marriage as a result of adultery is from God. We often fall into the trap of thinking that God *sends* the wrath because we confuse His *warnings* about the devastating consequences of sin with Him being the actual *cause* of those consequences. Yet when a mother warns a child against touching a hot stove, we do not think the mother is the one who sent the burn upon the child when the child touches the stove despite the mother's warnings. So also with God. He warns us about the wrath of disobedience, but is not the one who sends the wrath when we disobey. Wrath occurs quite naturally as a result of disobedience. Therefore, since "wrath" is a natural consequence of sin, "salvation" in Romans is to be delivered from the consequences of sin, which has far more to do with this life than with eternal life.

Once this understanding of "salvation" is recognized, we also see that this sort of deliverance is the overall *theme* of Romans.

Paul introduces the concept of salvation in Romans 1:16 by saying that the gospel is for the salvation of "those who believe," that
is, "for believers." Paul does not refer to salvation again until Romans 5:9, where he clearly states that salvation comes *after* justification. In other words, in Romans, salvation is something that
believers can experience *after* they have been justified. Paul's letter
to the Romans is all about the salvation of believers—that is, how
believers can live lives of significance in this world by living free
from sin so that we can serve God and others. This theme helps
bring together not only the chapters on sin and justification
(Romans 1–5), but also the chapters on sanctification and glorification (Romans 6–8), the chapters on God's calling and election
(Romans 9–11), and the chapters on living practically in this
world (Romans 12–16).

So "salvation" in Romans is about deliverance from wrath, or
deliverance from the consequences of sin. Yes, while there are
some eternal and spiritual consequences of sin, these are not
Paul's primary focus in this letter. Paul is writing to believers, and
is primarily concerned about how believers can be delivered from
wrath in this life. In his article on "Salvation in Romans," Bob
Wilkin writes this:

> It is my contention that the meaning of save and salvation in Ro-
> mans is consistent with its primary usage in the [New Testament].
> It doesn't refer to salvation from hell. It means deliverance from
> difficulties in this life. ... I am convinced that Romans discusses the

salvation of believers, not the salvation of unbelievers.[3]

In the rest of his article, Wilkin briefly considers all the various uses of the words "salvation" and "save" in Romans, showing that they do not refer to justification and eternal life, but to the deliverance from the damaging and destructive consequences of sin in the life of the believer.

All of this helps us understand how Romans 9–11 properly fits within the overall context of Romans, and more specifically, helps us understand the "salvation" references in Romans 9–11. Since "salvation" in Romans is not talking about eternal life, then "salvation" in Romans 9–11 is not about eternal life either. Hence, the discussions about election (Rom 9:10-24), God hardening Pharaoh's heart (Rom 9:17), calling on the name of the Lord to be saved (Rom 10:9-14), and the salvation of all Israel (Rom 11:26), are not about eternal life, but about living lives of service to God and others.

This leads to the second main key to understanding Romans 9:10-24. Since salvation is not about eternal life, what is Paul saying when he writes about election?

---

[3] Bob Wilkin, "Salvation in Romans," *Grace in Focus Newsletter* (July-August 2014). http://www.faithalone.org/magazine/y2014/SALVATION-in-Romans.pdf Last Accessed January 1, 2015.

CHAPTER 2

ELECTION IS TO SERVICE

Many Calvinists recognize that according to the way they understand Romans 9–11, these three chapters do not really seem to fit the overall theme or thought flow of Romans. As mentioned earlier, Ernst Käsemann's admission that Romans 9–11 could be removed from Romans without any serious risk to the message of Romans indicates that scholars like Käsemann have pretty seriously misunderstood not only Romans 9–11, but the entire letter to the Romans as a whole.[1]

If, however, we grasp that the purpose of Romans is to teach believers how to be delivered from the devastating consequences of sin so they can serve God and others with their lives, then the discussion of election in Romans 9 not only fits within Paul's purpose for writing, but becomes absolutely essential to his letter. Paul has been arguing in Romans 1–8 that God has justified and sanctified a particular people for Himself so that they can live according to His purpose (Rom 8:28). He concludes chapter 8 by saying that nothing whatsoever can get in the way of this purpose

---

[1] As mentioned previously, Käsemann is a Lutheran, but his words represent the view of many Calvinists regarding Romans 9.

(Rom 8:31-39). The obvious objection to this, however, concerns the nation of Israel. Did not God also call Israel to live according to His purpose? Was not the nation of Israel God's chosen people to represent Him and serve others in this world? Yet it seems as if God's promises to them had failed. If God's word to Israel failed, then what reassurances do Christians have that God's word to us will not also fail? If we are called to serve the world, just as Israel was, but nothing can separate us from this purpose, then how is it that Israel was separated from theirs? It is this question that Paul answers in Romans 9–11.

Paul's basic answer is this: Israel was not set aside; they are still serving the purpose to which God called them. The church has not replaced Israel in God's plan for the world, but has been grafted in to supplement God's plan, which, as it turns out, was God's plan from the very beginning. And while it appears as if Israel has lost her way, she really has not, for the day is coming when Israel will return to her true calling, which will result in the resurrection of the world (cf. Rom 11:12-15). The entire discussion in Romans 9–11 is about God's calling and purpose for His people, whether they are Israel or the Church, and how His dealings with these two groups prove His sovereignty over all and faithfulness in keeping His promises.

> What was the nature and purpose of this divine election of Israel? I answer that Paul conceives of it as a historic action of God in setting apart the Jewish nation to a special mission or function in the world as the bearer of his revelation to all mankind. ... These chapters (Romans 9–11) treat of election to a historic function or mission, not of election to eternal destiny. ... Theology has often ap-

plied these ideas to the subject of man's final destiny. Whatever may be the logic of such an application, it is exegetically unjustifiable.[2]

This again points to the fact that the "election" in Romans 9 is not to eternal life, but to service. Just as God elected Israel to serve His purposes in the world, so also, God chose the Church for similar purposes. This understanding of election greatly helps us understand some notoriously difficult texts in Romans 9–11.

For example, Paul writes in Romans 11:17-21 that the elect branches were cut off so that non-elect branches could be grafted in, which in turn will lead to the elect-which-became-non-elect to be re-grafted back in and become re-elect. If Paul is referring to eternal life when he speaks of election, none of this makes any sense. How can a people or a nation whom God elected "to eternal life" before the foundation of the world go from being elect to non-elect and then re-elect? However, this makes perfect sense when we recognize that election is not to eternal life but to service. God wants to bless the world through His people, and if one group of people fails in this God-given task, then God will simply find someone else to do it while He continues to lead the first group to fulfill His overarching purposes—albeit in different ways than originally intended. If this second group also fails, they too will be moved into an alternative role in accomplishing God's will (Rom 11:17-21). If necessary, God could raise up a people for Himself from rocks (Matt 3:9). In this way, when Paul writes

---

[2] George B. Stevens, *The Theology of the New Testament* (Edinburgh: T&T Clark, 1918), 380-386.

about branches being cut off so others can be grated in which will lead to the cut off branches being grafted back in again, he is not talking about people losing and regaining eternal life, but about losing and re-gaining places of privilege and purpose in God's plan for this world. God's plan of redemption started with Israel, shifted to the Gentiles, and eventually will reincorporate Israel so that "of Him and through Him and to Him are all things" (Rom 11:36).

This understanding of election to service also helps make sense of Romans 11:32: "For God has committed them all to disobedience, that He might have mercy on all." If we understand Paul to be talking about giving eternal life to people, then it seems from this text that Paul is saying that all people will receive eternal life. Paul would then be teaching some form of universalism. Bible scholars who understand Paul to be referring to eternal life go to great lengths to explain that when Paul says "all" he doesn't mean "all without exception" but rather "all without distinction." This argument is often found in the Calvinistic doctrine of Limited Atonement, but regarding Romans 11:32, Calvinists say that God doesn't actually show mercy to *all* people, for then all people would receive eternal life. Instead, they say that God shows mercy to all *kinds of* people, or to *some people* from all tongues, tribes, and nations.[3] But if we remain consistent with the theme of salvation in Romans as not referring to justification or receiving eter-

---

[3] See, for example, the debate between James White and Michael Brown. http://www.aomin.org/podcasts/20100325.mp3   Go here for a partial transcript: http://www.examiningcalvinism.com/files/Paul/Romans11_32.html Last Accessed January 2, 2015.

nal life, this then helps us understand what Paul is talking about in Romans 11:32. We can take Paul's words at face value without becoming Universalists, for God can easily show mercy to all people without exception by staying His hand of judgment and inviting them to participate in His plan and purposes for the world. This understanding is further supported by the explanation of Romans 9:23 in the section about the potter and the clay, which will be looked at below.

Seeing that Romans 9–11 are not about who receives eternal life and who does not helps us better understand Paul's message in these critical chapters, and also helps us better place them within the overall context of Paul's letter. The discussion of election in Romans 9 has nothing whatsoever to do with election to eternal life, but rather with election to service. "This chapter is about corporate election to service, not individual election to eternal life."[4]

Numerous highly-regarded Bible scholars and theologians agree that in Romans 9, election is to service. In his commentary on Romans, W. H. Griffith Thomas wrote this:

> The primary thought of the apostle in these chapters is not individual salvation, but the philosophy of history. … Israel's election had for its object the service of his fellow men. St. Paul is concerned not so much with individuals, as with nations and masses of people. He speaks of God's choice of Israel, not to eternal life as such, but to

---

[4] Lazar, "Election for Baptists," 7.

privileges and duty. ... God's chosen men are His 'choice' men.[5]

Both Romans commentaries in the *International Critical Commentary* series have the same approach:

> We must not read into it more than it contains: as, for example, Calvin does. He imports various extraneous ideas. ... The apostle says nothing about eternal life or death.[6]

> The assumption that Paul is here thinking of the ultimate destiny of the individual, of his final salvation or final ruin, is not justified by the text.[7]

Harry Ironside, that great expositor and preacher, wrote this in his book, *Lectures on Romans:*

> There is no question here of predestination to heaven or reprobation to hell; in fact, eternal issues do not really come in throughout this chapter. ... We are not told here, nor anywhere else, that before children are born it is God's purpose to send one to heaven and another to hell. ... The passage has to do entirely with privilege here on earth.[8]

---

[5] W. H. Griffith Thomas, *Commentary on Romans* (Grand Rapids: Kregel, 1974), 115-116, 156-157, 222, 228-229.

[6] William Sanday and Arthur C. Headlam, *Romans*, International Critical Commentary (Edinburgh: T&T Clark, 1902), 258.

[7] C. E. B. Cranfield, *A Critical and Exegetical Commentary on the Epistles to the Romans*, Reprinted with corrections. ed., 2 vols., The International Critical Commentary (Edinburgh: T&T Clark, 1975-79), 2:489.

[8] H. A. Ironside, *Lectures on the Epistle to the Romans* (New York: Loizeaux Brothers, 1927), 109-110, 116.

J. Sidlow Baxter wrote similarly in his classic introduction to the Bible, *Explore the Book*:

> As to the scope of the passage, it will become obvious that it is all about God's dealings with men and nations historically and dispensationally, and is not about individual salvation and destiny beyond the grave. Now that is the absolutely vital fact to remember in reading the problem verses of these chapters. John Calvin is wrong when he reads into these verses election either to salvation or to damnation in the eternal sense. That is not their scope. They belong only to a divine economy of history. ... Let us further say that God could never create any man either to be wicked or to be eternally damned. 'Is there unrighteousness with God? God forbid!' In Romans 9 we simply must not read an after-death significance into what is solely historical.[9]

Finally, Greek scholar and author M. R. Vincent wrote this:

> These chapters, as they are the most difficult of Paul's writings, have been most misunderstood and misapplied. Their most dangerous perversion is that which draws from them the doctrine of God's arbitrary predestination of individuals to eternal life or eternal perdition. It can be shown that such is not the intent of these chapters. They do not discuss the doctrine of individual election and reprobation with reference to eternal destiny.[10]

John Piper is aware of the view that Romans 9 is not about

---

[9] J. Sidlow Baxter, *Explore the Book* (Grand Rapids: Zondervan, 1986), VI:88-89.

[10] Marvin R. Vincent, *Word Studies in the New Testament*, 4 vols. (Peabody, MA: Hendrickson, 1985), III:133-135.

election to eternal life but election to service, but argues against this view based on Paul's words in Romans 9:2-3 where Paul writes that he has unceasing anguish in his heart for his fellow Israelites who are cut off from Christ.[11] For Piper, this is an indication that Paul is primarily concerned with the eternal destiny of the Israelite people. Yet Paul clearly explains in Romans 9:4 what he is referring to regarding Israel being cut off. It is not their *eternal life* Paul has in view—for any Israelite may receive eternal life through faith in Jesus (cf. Rom 11:1-25)—but their adoption, glory, covenants, law, service, and promises (Rom 9:4). Paul is concerned that his fellow Israelites are not living up to their God-given purpose in this world to which they have been called. God adopted Israel and gave her the law and covenants so that they could serve Him by being a blessing to the world. Even in Romans 9:2-3, election is to service.

In light of all this, we can see how Romans 9 follows logically from Romans 8, and therefore, how Paul's point in Romans 8 stands true. When it comes to bringing those who are in Christ by faith to glorification, there is nothing that can get in God's way. He has decided from eternity past to bring to glorification all those who are justified. But this does not mean, as Paul points out in Romans 9–11, that if we fail to serve God or live up to our purpose in life, He won't elect someone else who will. Bringing His children to glory and calling His children to serve Him are

---

[11] John Piper, *Five Points: Toward a Deeper Understanding of God's Grace* (Geanies House, Scotland: Christian Focus, 2014), 55. See a longer treatment of Romans 9 in John Piper, *The Justification of God: An Exegetical and Theological Study of Romans 9:1-23* (Grand Rapids: Baker, 1983).

two separate issues. All who are justified will be glorified, but not all who are justified will always serve God faithfully. Yet when God's people do not serve as He plans or intends, this does not thwart God. He is infinitely wise and resourceful. God wants to bless the world through His people, but if His people will not be a blessing to the world, God finds other people who will. And depending on what specifically God is seeking to accomplish, He can elect either individual people or entire nations and people groups. This is the next key which helps us understand Paul's teaching on election in Romans 9.

CHAPTER 3

ELECTION IS CORPORATE
AND INDIVIDUAL

There is a long-standing debate about election, regarding whether Paul is talking about corporate election or individual election. That is, when Paul writes about the election of Israel, or God's choice of Jacob over Esau, is Paul talking about the individuals within Israel, and the individual destinies of Jacob and Esau, or is Paul referring instead to the national and corporate destinies of Israel (which came from Jacob) and Edom (which came from Esau)? Usually, the battle lines over this debate are determined by whether a person is a Calvinist or not. As Calvinists believe and teach the individual election of certain people to eternal life, they are more likely to understand and explain Romans 9 in this light. Those who do not hold to Calvinism tend to interpret Romans 9 as teaching corporate election. Henry Halley, author of *Halley's Bible Handbook,* is one such writer:

> Paul is not discussing the predestination of individuals to salvation

or condemnation, but is asserting God's absolute sovereignty in the choice and management of nations for world functions.[1]

So which is it? Is Paul talking about individual election or corporate election? The stance taken here is that Paul is teaching *both* corporate and individual election. Since it is the purposes of God that determine who gets elected and to what form of service they are elected, then it is God who decides when He needs to call individuals and when He needs to call nations or groups of people to perform certain tasks. Of course, even when election is corporate, it is true that God's purpose for that group of people is carried out by individuals within the group, and so in this sense, we can say that even corporate election has an individual aspect. On the other hand, the benefit to corporate election is that even if some individuals within the corporate identity do not contribute to fulfill the purpose of the corporate entity, there will be some within the group that will fulfill their purpose, thus accomplishing God's purpose in election.

Nevertheless, it sometimes happens that the failure of individuals occurs on a large scale. This is what happened to Israel, and which concerns Paul in Romans 9–11. Paul's point in these chapters is that even when God's purposes for an elect nation fail, God's overall purposes are not thwarted; He simply finds another way to accomplish His will. In the case of Israel not fulfilling her corporate calling, God pursued multiple alternative options, which Paul explains in Romans 9–11.

---

[1] Henry Hampton Halley, *Halley's Bible Handbook: An Abbreviated Bible Commentary*, 24th ed. (Grand Rapids: Zondervan, 1965), 527.

First, Paul states that despite the widespread failure of Israel as a nation, many individuals within Israel were still fulfilling their elected purpose. The Jewish prophets and Paul himself are examples (Rom 9:2-5). Such Jewish believers are "elect" within the "elect."[2] They are the elect according to grace (Rom 11:5-7; cf. 4:14-16) who are also part of the elect according to the flesh. It is important to note as well, as Robert Shank does in his book *Elect in the Son,* that while Romans 11:5 certainly teaches that election is not of works, this does not prove that election is unconditional. All it establishes is that election is by grace, and not by works.[3] Though election is to service, it is still by grace.

Second, even when God's purpose in electing a particular person or nation fails, the purpose of God *itself* does not fail, for God sovereignly accomplishes His plan and purposes by electing other individuals or nations to accomplish His will. This is the meaning of Paul's discussion about the tree and the branches in Romans 11:13-32.

Finally, Paul goes out of his way to point out that God's purpose in election is not limited only to "His people" or to people who are justified by faith. He mentions how God chose the older son to serve the younger son (Rom 9:12), God chose Pharaoh to serve His purpose (Rom 9:17), and in alluding to Jeremiah's illustration of the potter and the clay reminds the people that God raised up King Cyrus to accomplish His will (Rom 9:21). We will

---

[2] Roger Forster and Paul Marston, *God's Strategy in Human History* (Eugene, OR: Wipf and Stock, 2000), 142.

[3] Robert Shank, *Elect in the Son; A Study of the Doctrine of Election* (Springfield, MO: Westcott, 1970), 125.

return to these three examples from Paul in the next three sections.

By taking the approach that Paul is thinking of *both* corporate *and* individual election, we can avoid the missteps of those who come down on one side of the issue or the other. For example, in his commentary on Romans, Douglas Moo takes the position that Paul is teaching about individual election. In his discussion, Moo raises many sound objections to the idea that Paul is referring only to the corporate election of Israel in Romans 9.[4] Moo is right that Paul cannot be referring only to corporate election. The problem, however, is that Moo transitions from the arguments for individual election to the claim that this individual election is to eternal life (which he calls salvation).[5] This is the primary problem with thinking that the election of Romans 9 is only of individuals. Along with Moo, a great number of commentators on Romans have incorrectly defined "salvation" in Romans as being equivalent to receiving eternal life.[6] This "misdefinition" of salvation then leads to much confusion about what Paul writes in Romans 9–11 about individual and corporate election.

But when we see that Paul is teaching *both* individual and corporate election, we are then liberated to understand that elec-

---

[4] Douglas J. Moo, *The Epistle to the Romans*, ed. F.F. Bruce Ned B. Stonehouse, & Gordon D. Fee, The New International Commentary on the New Testament (Grand Rapids: Eerdmans, 1996), 570f.

[5] Cf. Ibid., 571.

[6] Cf. the similar statement by John Murray: "The interpretation which regards the election as the collective, theocratic election of Israel as a people must be rejected and 'the purpose of God according to election' will have to be understood as the electing purpose that is determinative of and unto salvation." See John Murray, *Epistle to the Romans* (Grand Rapids: Eerdmans, 1965), 2:19.

tion cannot be to eternal life (for it is impossible that all individuals of a particular nation will be justified), and will instead see
that election is to service. Once this is grasped, many of the con-
fusing texts in Romans 9 make more sense in light of Paul's overall argument in Romans 9–11 and the letter of Romans as a
whole. It is to these texts we now turn, beginning with God's
choice of Jacob and Esau.

CHAPTER 4

GOD'S CHOICE OF JACOB AND ESAU (ROMANS 9:10-13)

It may be shocking to realize that God chose both Jacob *and* Esau. Most studies and commentaries on Roman 9 will say that God chose Jacob *instead of* Esau. Those which recognize that God chose both Jacob and Esau are usually written by Calvinistic scholars who want to teach double predestination, so that Jacob was chosen by God for justification and eternal life while Esau was chosen by God for reprobation and eternal damnation. Ernst Käsemann, a Lutheran scholar, was quoted before, but his statement is appropriate here as well:

> ... only here does Paul present double-predestination. Not until this is admitted without reserve can one see its necessary delimitations and ask about its significance within the framework of the apostle's theology.[1]

Many Calvinists concur, such as A. W. Pink and R. C. Sproul,

---

[1] Ernst Käsemann and Geoffrey William Bromiley, *Commentary on Romans* (Grand Rapids: Eerdmans, 1980), 265.

Jr.[2] Such authors see from the text that both Jacob and Esau were chosen by God, but believing as they do that election is to eternal life (or eternal death), conclude that Jacob was chosen for redemption and Esau was chosen for damnation.

We can, however, agree with the Calvinists that both Jacob and Esau were "chosen" by God, while disagreeing with the Calvinists that God chose one for eternal life and the other for eternal damnation. Instead, since election is to service, God chose one to perform one type of service, and the other for a different type.

Paul begins his discussion in Romans 9:6 by stating that "they are not all Israel who are of Israel." When we remember that "Israel" is another name for "Jacob," Paul's point becomes clear. He is saying two things: that not all who are physical descendants from Jacob are members of the nation of Israel and not all who are members of the nation of Israel can trace their lineage back to Jacob. One example of what Paul is referring to is when the Israelites left Egypt. When they left, some Israelites stayed in Egypt because they did not want to abandon the positions of relative power and influence they had gained in Egypt, while at the same time, many Egyptians left Egypt and joined with Israel in the Exodus (Exod 12:38).[3] In so doing, the Israelites who stayed behind essentially became Egyptians, and the Egyptians who went with Israel essentially became Israelites. Similar shifts occurred at vari-

---

[2] See A. W. Pink, *The Sovereignty of God* (Grand Rapids: Baker, 1930); A. W. Pink, *The Doctrines of Election and Justification* (Grand Rapids: Baker, 1974); R. C. Sproul Jr., *Almighty Over All: Understanding the Sovereignty of God* (Grand Rapids: Baker, 1999).

[3] Jewish tradition teaches that only one-fifth of all Israelites left Egypt. See Rashi on Exodus 10:22; 13:18.

ous times throughout Israelite history. The Samaritans were a contemporary example in the days of Jesus and Paul. Not all national Israelites are descendants of Jacob, and not all who are descendants of Jacob are part of national Israel.

In Romans 9:7, Paul writes that this separation of some physical descendants from the national identity began from the very beginning of Israel with Abraham himself. Abraham had two sons, Ishmael and Isaac, and yet God said, "In Isaac your seed shall be called." So here also, not all who are physical descendants of Abraham were called by God to fulfill the purpose for which God chose and called Abraham. This does not mean that Ishmael and his descendants are accursed or cut off from God, for God also promised to bless him, multiply his people, and make him into a great nation (Gen 17:20). Yet the blessing of God upon Ishmael was different than the blessing God had in store for Isaac.

Paul's point is that it is the children of the promise that fulfill God's covenant to Abraham; not the children of the flesh (Rom 9:8). Again, since the promise to Abraham was that in him all the world would be blessed (Gen 12:3), there is nothing in Paul's words about the eternal destiny of either type of Abraham's descendants. Paul does not say that all of Isaac's descendants will end up in heaven while all of Ishmael's will end up in hell. The same is true of the descendants of Jacob and Esau. The promise and covenant of God to Abraham through Isaac and Jacob has to do with how God will bring blessing to the world; not how one group of people will receive eternal life while the other receives eternal damnation.

The quotation from Malachi 1:2-3 confirms that Paul refers not to personal salvation, but to God's choice of the nation Israel over Edom. Hence, Jacob and Esau represent their progeny. In tracing the ancestry of the Jews, Paul asserts that God chose an individual—Jacob—for a specific mission or task, as he had chosen Isaac and Abraham before him. [4]

Paul goes on to explain that just as the promise of the covenants went through Isaac instead of Ishmael, so also the promise went through Jacob instead of Esau (Rom 9:10-13). Note carefully what Paul does and does not say in these verses. As Paul is only talking about how the promise of the covenant went through Isaac and Jacob instead of through Ishmael and Esau, Paul is saying absolutely nothing about the eternal destinies of any one of these four individuals, let alone the eternal destinies of all their descendants. Nor does Paul say anything about Ishmael and Esau not being chosen. To the contrary, the way Paul structures his argument and Old Testament quotations, he seems to be saying that while Isaac and Jacob were chosen to be recipients of the promise, Ishmael and Esau were still chosen by God, but for other purposes and tasks. This is especially true when we consider Romans 9:12: "The older shall serve the younger." In other words, God *chose* Esau to *serve* Jacob. Since God's choosing and election in Romans 9 is not to eternal life, but to vocation, mission, purpose, and service, here we see that Esau was elected to service! It certainly was a different service than the one to which Jacob was called, but it is clearly a call to service nonetheless. This

---

[4] William W. Klein, *The New Chosen People: A Corporate View of Election* (Eugene, OR: Wipf and Stock, 1990), 198.

call to various forms of service was not only true of the individuals, Esau and Jacob, but also to the nations that came from them, Edom and Israel. Just as Israel was chosen to perform a particular type of service to the world, so also Edom was chosen to perform a particular type of service to Israel.

This leads to the difficult statement in Romans 9:13: "Jacob I have loved, but Esau I have hated." Scholars debate whether or not God actually hated Esau. Some argue that the reference to hate in Malachi 1:2-3 is a Hebrew idiom for "love less." They point out that Jesus instructs us to love our enemies rather than hate them (Matt 5:44), point to the places where Jesus tells His disciples to both hate and love their parents (Luke 14:26; Mark 10:19), and remind people that God has strictly forbidden the Israelites from hating the Edomites (Deut 23:7). Greg Boyd succinctly explains this idea:

> Some might suppose that God's pronouncement that he "loved" Jacob and "hated" Esau shows that he is speaking about their individual eternal destinies, but this is mistaken. In Hebraic thought, when "love" and "hate" are contrasted they usually are meant hyperbolically. The expression simply means to strongly prefer one person or thing over another.
>
> So, for example, when Jesus said, "Whoever comes to me and does not hate father and mother, wife and children, brothers and sisters, yes, and even life itself, cannot be my disciple" (Lk 14:26), he was not saying we should literally hate these people. Elsewhere he taught people to love and respect their parents, as the Old Testament also taught (Mk 10:19). Indeed, he commanded us to love even our enemies (Mt 5:44)! What Jesus was saying was that he must be preferred above parents, spouses, children, siblings and

even life itself. The meaning of Malachi's phrase, then, is simply that God preferred Israel over Edom to be the people he wanted to work with to reach out to the world.[5]

Others, however, argue that God did in fact hate Esau (and the Edomites), for that is what the text clearly states. The Calvinistic commentator John Murray provides a good explanation of this view:

> We must, therefore, recognize that there is in God a holy hate that cannot be defined in terms of not loving or loving less. Furthermore, we may not tone down the reality of intensity of this hate by speaking of it as "anthropopathic" ... The case is rather, as in all virtue, that this holy hate in us is patterned after holy hate in God.[6]

So which view is right? Does God hate Esau and Edom, or does He simply *love* Edom *less* than He loves Israel?

The solution to the problem of Romans 9:13 is to agree with those who say that "hate" means "hate," but to also agree with the others who argue that neither Paul nor Malachi are talking about Esau's eternal destiny (or anyone else for that matter). More critical still is to recognize that what God hated is *not specifically Esau*, for Malachi 1:3 was written many centuries after he had died, nor was God saying He hates the *people* of Edom. Instead, God hated how Edom *behaved* toward Israel. The Hebrew word used in

---

[5] Greg Boyd, "How do you respond to Romans 9?" http://reknew.org/2008/01/how-do-you-respond-to-romans-9/ Last Accessed January 3, 2015.

[6] John Murray, *Epistle to the Romans* (Grand Rapids: Eerdmans, 1965), 2:22.

Malachi 1:3 for "hate" (Heb., *sanati*) is used in various other places to speak of hatred for the sin and wickedness of people (cf. Psa 26:5; 101:3; 119:104, 128, 163; Prov 8:13; Jer 44:3; Amos 5:21; 6:8; Zech 8:17), not hatred for the people themselves. In light of what many other biblical prophets say about the actions and behavior of Edom (cf. Jer 49:7-22; Lam 4:21-22; Ezek 25:12-14; Amos 1:6-11), this is how we can understand God's hatred in Malachi 1:3. God does not hate Edom; He hates how she has behaved. Specifically, God hated how Edom treated Israel.

What makes this approach interesting is that God's hatred for the sinful actions of Edom arose because of the evil things the nation had done. God had chosen Esau to serve Jacob, but Esau completely failed in this service. Though chosen to serve Israel, Edom chose to rebel instead. This began with Esau himself.

> Not only does the text not say "the elder shall be lost and the younger shall be saved," Esau as an individual never served Jacob; the very opposite happened. Jacob bowed down to Esau (Gen 33:3), called him lord (Gen 33:8), claimed to be his servant (Gen 33:5), and urged him to accept gifts (Gen 33:11).[7]

This failure by Esau to serve his brother became a pattern for the nation of Edom. Edom deserted Israel, abandoned her, and even gloated over her when she was destroyed and sold into slavery. For this reason, God's choice that Esau would serve Jacob resulted in God's choice that Edom would be destroyed (Mal 1:4).

---

[7] Laurence M. Vance, *The Other Side of Calvinism* (Pensacola, FL: Vance Publications, 1999), 322.

Paul's point is this: Before Jacob or Esau had done anything good or bad—indeed, before either one was even born—God chose Jacob to carry the promise and chose Esau to serve Jacob. But in refusing to serve the descendants of Jacob and in betraying Israel instead, the descendants of Esau performed much evil and their sin brought wrath down upon them to their destruction. Before either Jacob or Esau had done anything good or bad, God made some choices about how each would serve His purposes on earth. But as a result of Edom's great evil, they lost the opportunity to serve as God intended. Paul's point here is the same point he has had throughout Romans: sin brings devastation and destruction. If we want to live up to our potential and fulfill our purpose, we must seek to live free from sin.

None of this means that any particular individual within Edom is outside of God's favor or beyond the reaches of God's grace. Paul is not saying that either Esau individually or that all Edomites corporately are destined for eternal damnation. Quite to the contrary, any Edomite had just as much opportunity to believe and receive eternal life from God as anyone within Israel. God chose Israel so that they might be a blessing to the surrounding nations—including Edom! Just as the heavens declare the glory of God, so also, God's chosen people are to declare the glory of God and call all people to respond to Him in faith. The prophet Amos understood this, which is why he specifically mentions that in the last days, the remnant of Edom will join with other Gentiles who are called by God's name and join with God's people in worshiping Him in His holy temple (Amos 9:11-12). Even Edom is within God's redemptive purposes.

CHAPTER 5

THE RAISING UP AND HARDENING OF PHARAOH (ROMANS 9:14-18)

What then of Pharaoh? If Esau and his descendants also were potentially within the redemptive purposes of God, could this also be true of Pharaoh and the Egyptians? If God is as gracious and long-suffering as Paul claims, then how could it *not* be so? Nevertheless, the storm that rages around the issue of the hardening of Pharaoh's heart has left much damage in its wake. Countless hours have been spent, papers written, and books published around this single issue.

Usually, the debate centers on the age-old scholarly debate about who hardened Pharaoh's heart first. In this debate, Calvinists say that God hardened Pharaoh's heart first from eternity past because God needed a vessel of destruction through whom to reveal His wrath. They say that the text is quite clear in teaching that God hardened Pharaoh's heart (Exod 9:12; 10:1, 20, 27; 11:10; 14:4, 8). Non-Calvinists respond that in the Exodus account, the text frequently states that Pharaoh hardened his own heart before God hardened it (8:15, 32; 9:34). There are also several references which state that Pharaoh's heart was hardened without giving indication about the source of this hardening

(7:13, 14, 22; 8:19; 9:7, 35). But in response to this, Calvinists argue back that although the text says that Pharaoh hardened his own heart before God hardened it, before Moses even went to speak to Pharaoh, God told Him that He planned to harden Pharaoh's heart (Exod 4:21; 7:3). As one is reading all the exegetical and theological arguments surrounding this debate about who hardened Pharaoh's heart first, it begins to sound a bit like the question of which came first: the chicken or the egg.

Rather than summarizing all the exegetical and theological arguments on both sides of this debate, it seems best to avoid all the rhetoric and cut through to the main question which neither side seems to be asking. The question is this: "What does it *mean* for Pharaoh's heart to be hardened?" The issue is not about who hardened Pharaoh's heart first—though that is where most of the ink has been spilt—but rather about what it *means* for Pharaoh's heart to be hardened. People on both sides of the debate often assume that the hardening of Pharaoh's heart means that Pharaoh was *solidified* in his status as an *unregenerate person* headed for hell. But what if the hardening of Pharaoh's heart doesn't mean this at all? What if it simply refers instead to the resolve in Pharaoh's heart to keep the Israelites as his slaves, and has absolutely nothing whatsoever to do with Pharaoh's eternal destiny? What if God, in His desire to make His glory known to both the Israelites and the Egyptians, made certain that Pharaoh would resist the will of God to deliver the people of Israel from Egypt, so that all those who witnessed and heard of these events would know that the God of Israel alone was God? Could not God, in His gracious sovereignty, do such a thing with Pharaoh without affecting whatsoever Pharaoh's ability to believe in God's promises and thus become part of God's redeemed people? Of course He could! Dr. J. Sidlow Baxter makes a similar point:

> The awesome words to Pharaoh can be faced in their full force—"Even for this same purpose have I raised thee up, that I might show My power in thee, and that My name might be declared throughout all the earth." The words "raised thee up" do not mean that God had raised him up from birth for this purpose: they refer to his elevation to the highest throne on earth. Nay, as they occur in Exodus 9:16, they scarce mean even that, but only that God had kept Pharaoh from dying in the preceding plague, so as to be made the more fully an object lesson to all men. Moreover, when Paul (still alluding to Pharaoh) says, "And whom He will, He hardeneth" (Exod 9:18), we need not try to soften the word. God did not override Pharaoh's own will. The hardening was a reciprocal process. Eighteen times we are told that Pharaoh's heart was "hardened" in refusal. In about half of these the hardening is attributed to Pharaoh himself; in the others to God. But the whole contest between God and Pharaoh must be interpreted by what God said to Moses before ever the contest started: "The king of Egypt will not" (Exod 3:19). The will was already set. The heart was already hard. The hardening process developed inasmuch as the plagues forced Pharaoh to an issue which crystallized his sin. ... Pharaoh's eternal destiny is not the thing in question.[1]

This means that the hardening of Pharaoh's heart, whether it is done by God or Pharaoh, or by some symbiotic combination of the two, has absolutely nothing to do with Pharaoh's eternal des-

---

[1] J. Sidlow Baxter, *Explore the Book* (Grand Rapids: Zondervan, 1986), VI:88-89.

tiny. Even if the Exodus account laid all the responsibility for the hardening of Pharaoh's heart upon God Himself, and none upon Pharaoh, this still would tell us nothing about whether or not Pharaoh concluded His life as one of God's redeemed. Pharaoh's eternal destiny is not under discussion in Exodus or in Romans, and so Pharaoh's heart can be hardened so that God's purposes are achieved, while still leaving plenty of room for Pharaoh to believe in God's promises and become one of God's people.

> That the purpose to which Pharaoh was raised up and the subsequent hardening had nothing to do with Pharaoh's eternal destiny is perfectly clear ... Pharaoh was said to be raised up to show God's power—not to be damned to hell by a sovereign, eternal decree. The purpose being that God might prove to Israel that he was the Lord who delivered them (Exod 6:6-7; 10:1-2; 13:14-16), to show Pharaoh that he was the only God (Exod 9:14), to show the Egyptians that he was the Lord (Exod 7:5; 14:4, 18), and that his name might be declared throughout the whole earth (Exod 9:16).[2]

That this is how to understand the hardening of Pharaoh's heart is seen by comparing the events in Exodus with other examples of the hardening of hearts in Scripture. Nowhere in Scripture does the hardening of hearts have anything to do with a person's or nation's eternal destiny (cf. Rom 11:26-31; Isa 63:17). The primary reason some scholars and authors think hardening does refer a person's eternal destiny is because they do not under-

---

[2] Laurence M. Vance, *The Other Side of Calvinism* (Pensacola, FL: Vance Publications, 1999), 326.

stand Paul's use of the term "salvation" in Romans.[3] But as soon as we see that "salvation" in Romans has nothing to do with eternal destiny, then we are free to reconsider what it means for God to have hardened Pharaoh's heart. When we do this, we see that God's choice of Pharaoh is similar to God's choice of Judas. Both were chosen by God for a task. This task had nothing whatsoever to do with whether or not they were eternally damned, but instead had everything to do with God seeking to accomplish His will on earth. "Whether or not they receive salvation [i.e., eternal life] is an issue separate from their selection for a task."[4]

> God's actions on Pharaoh stimulated not so much impenitence as foolhardiness. The end effect was not about eternal destiny, but a place in God's strategy in his plans on this earth. … The "hardening" of Pharaoh and the "mercy" on Moses are not about them going to heaven or hell, but about their roles in those unfolding plans for Israel through whom "all nations of the earth will be blessed.[5]

Though it may be unlikely, I would not be too surprised to discover when I enter heaven that Pharaoh ended up believing what God had revealed to him through Israel, and as a result, is spending eternity with all of God's redeemed.[6]

---

[3] Cf. Douglas J. Moo, *The Epistle to the Romans*, ed. F.F. Bruce Ned B. Stonehouse, & Gordon D. Fee, The New International Commentary on the New Testament (Grand Rapids: Eerdmans, 1996), 597.

[4] William W. Klein, *The New Chosen People: A Corporate View of Election* (Eugene, OR: Wipf and Stock, 1990), 198.

[5] Roger Forster and Paul Marston, *God's Strategy in Human History* (Eugene, OR: Wipf and Stock, 2000), 63, 261.

[6] Judas too, for that matter? See Dale Taliaferro, *Judas and Divine Grace* (Kearney, NE: Equipped for Life Ministries, 2013).

In his excellent commentary on Exodus, Hebrew scholar Marcus Kalisch wrote this:

> The phrase "I shall harden the heart of Pharaoh" means: I know that I shall be the cause of Pharaoh's obstinacy—my commandments and wonders will be an occasion, an inducement to an increasing obduration of his heart. And the compassionate leniency of God, who, instead of crushing the haughtiness of the refractory king with one powerful blow, first tried to reform him by various less awful punishments, and who generally announced the time of the occurrence of the plagues by the words, "Behold I shall afflict tomorrow" in order to grant him time for reflection and repentance; this clemency on the part of God increased Pharaoh's refractoriness; it was to him a cause of prolonged and renewed resistance.[7]

So how was Pharaoh's heart hardened? It was hardened as all hearts are hardened: through personal pride and sinful rebellion. Pride and rebellion sees leniency, forbearance, forgiveness, and long-suffering as a weakness to be exploited, and in so doing, becomes more sin-hardened. God did not harden Pharaoh's heart by being cruel and mean, but by acting in the only way God can act. God has no other way of approaching sin and pride but through love, forgiveness, mercy, patience, long-suffering, kindness, and grace. These are at the heart of who God is and all God does. So when God told Moses that He would harden Pharaoh's heart, it was with deep sadness that God said this, for God knew that Pharaoh, seeing the mercy and forbearance of God, would

---

[7] Kalisch, cited in Forster and Marston, *God's Strategy*, 262. Cf. the notes from Alfred Edersheim on the same page.

only see such tenderness and patience as a weakness. It was not God's plan or desire to harden Pharaoh, but God knew that when He revealed His patient power to Pharaoh in the attempt to get Pharaoh to recognize Israel's God as the only true God, Pharaoh would only respond with greater pride and rebellion. Yet when Pharaoh's kingdom came crashing down around him through the Ten Plagues and the destruction of his army in the Red Sea, one wonders if Pharaoh learned the lesson God had sought to teach him, and had returned back to his empty throne room where he threw himself upon the mercy of the One True God, recognizing God's sovereignty and power over all—even over Pharaoh himself. The Bible does not say this happened, but we can hope.

CHAPTER 6

THE POTTER AND THE CLAY
(ROMANS 9:19-24)

Paul's discussion about Esau and Pharaoh leads him to summarize this section of his letter with the fundamental principle he is seeking to illustrate, namely, that God has the right to do with His creation whatever He wants. While this sort of idea initially seems to support the Calvinistic perspective on this passage that God can even decide which people to redeem for eternal life and which to condemn to eternal death, Paul's point is actually the opposite. While it is true, Paul points out, that God has the right to do with His creation whatever He wants, the things that God wants to do, Paul reiterates, are fully and completely within the loving, merciful, and gracious character of God. In other words, it is not that God chooses who will be redeemed and who will be condemned and we must accept His sovereign choice as merciful and loving, but rather that, from His sovereign character traits of being loving and merciful, God works in this world with all types of people to accomplish His plan and goals for this world, and in so doing, bring as many people as possible into His family. God does not create some people for reconciliation and others for reprobation. No, God sovereignly uses people as He finds them, with the goal of redeeming and reconciling all to Himself.

To show this, Paul uses the Old Testament illustration of the potter and the clay in Romans 9:19-24. To begin with, it is important to recognize that this section of Romans is another example of Paul's rhetorical use of epistolary diatribe argumentation. In other words, Paul is allowing an imaginary objector to state his opposition to Paul's argument before Paul refutes what the objector is saying. So the question in Romans 9:19 "Who can resist God's will?" does not come from Paul, but from someone who disagrees with Paul. As such, I often find it interesting when Calvinists quote Romans 9:19 to defend their position, for in so doing, they are actually quoting a person who objects to what Paul teaches.[1] It is not Paul, but the person who objects to Paul's argument, who believes that nobody can resist God's will. When the Calvinist argues that nobody can resist God's will, the Calvinist is not agreeing with Paul, but with the person who disagrees with Paul.

The objection in Romans 9:19 rises because of what Paul wrote about Pharaoh in Romans 9:14-18. Paul has stated that Pharaoh became the way he was because God wanted Pharaoh to be hardened so that God could reveal His character and power to Israel and to Egypt. Again, this had nothing whatsoever to do with Pharaoh's eternal destiny, but relates only to Pharaoh's ac-

---

[1] Forster and Marston, *God's Strategy*, 71. Douglas Campbell takes a slightly different track, but still allows the Jewish imaginary objector to become entrapped by Paul's rhetorical logic. See Douglas A Campbell, *The Deliverance of God: An Apocalyptic Rereading of Justificatin in Paul* (Grand Rapids: Eerdmans, 2009), 776-777.

tions in resisting God at the time of the Israelite Exodus from Egypt.

In light of this, the person who objects to Paul claims that in such a case, Pharaoh could not have been held liable for his behavior, because nobody can resist God's will. How can God "still find fault?" the objector asks, "For who has resisted His will?" In other words, the objector believes that everything occurs because God wills it to occur—including Pharaoh's rebellion against God. This sounds startlingly similar to the Calvinistic insistence on the complete sovereignty of God over all things, including the falling of a leaf, the lifting of a finger, and the writing of a letter with a pen.[2]

In Romans 9:20, Paul sets out to answer this objection. Note carefully what this means. The fact the Paul seeks to refute an imaginary objector who believes that no one can resist God's will, means that Paul himself believes that people can *and do* resist God's will. Exhibit A for Paul is the objector himself. Using a bit of light irony, Paul says, "Who are you to reply against God?" Paul has pointed out from Scripture that Pharaoh's heart was hardened by God and by his own response to God. When the objector states (through the pen of Paul) that Pharaoh should not have been found guilty for no one can resist God's will, Paul humorously points out that the objector himself is resisting God! Paul is saying, "You say that Pharaoh should not be held accountable for his actions because people cannot resist God's will? You

[2] Cf. Edwin H. Palmer, *The Five Points of Calvinism*, Enl. ed. (Grand Rapids: Baker, 1980), 25.

are resisting God's will right now by questioning what God did with Pharaoh!" As Paul Marston and Roger Forster point out, "The critic is a living demonstration that his criticism is nonsense!"[3]

This is a brilliant move by Paul, for it not only defends God's ability to harden Pharaoh's heart while at the same time holding Pharaoh accountable for hardening his own heart, Paul is now able to use this point to return to his overall theme of why and how God has now turned to the Gentiles to fulfill His strategy on earth. Though Paul has used the negative examples of Esau and Pharaoh, the objection of his Jewish interlocutor allows Paul to turn the argument back toward the Jewish people themselves. Paul has been arguing up to this point that God raised up the people of Israel to accomplish a particular function in His plan for the world, but because the Israelites failed in their God-given mission, God grafted the Gentiles in to this plan so that they might carry God's plan forward. By objecting that Pharaoh could only do what God had raised him up to do, the deterministic Jewish objector is also implying that the Jewish people only did what God wanted *them* to do, and hence, "He shouldn't blame us! We can only do what He wills!" In response, Paul gently mocks this objector by saying, "Really? You just told God what He should and should not do. If you are right that we can only do what God ordains, then you have no right to argue with God in how He grafted the Gentiles in to His plan."

What is Paul saying? "The claim that Paul is making here [is]

[3] Forster and Marston, *God's Strategy*, 72.

that the people of God now can legitimately include pagans should God wish to call them."[4] The Jewish objector is upset that God has included the Gentiles in to His plan of redemption, because the Jewish people only "failed" because they could only do what God determined, and furthermore, the Gentiles were not worthy to be included in God's plan. Paul disagrees with these points from the deterministic Jewish objector and argues instead that God does not determine or control people's lives, but works with people as He finds them to accomplish His purposes. In His wisdom, He is still able to accomplish His will, but He does so without compromising the divine gift of freedom which He bestowed upon humanity. God does not make people what they are, but works with people as they are. This allows Him to accomplish His will, while still holding people responsible for their own decisions and actions. This was true for Esau and Edom as it was for Pharaoh and Egypt. This is also true for Jews and Gentiles.

But Paul's point becomes even more glorious in his statements that follow. One objection that the Jewish people had to God using the Gentiles for His purposes is that the Gentiles were … well … Gentiles. It is as if the Jewish people were saying, "God cannot use *Gentiles* to accomplish His purposes on earth, can He? He must use His chosen people, the Jews!"

Paul has just shown that God's work in this world can be accomplished by people like Esau and Pharaoh, or the nations of Edom and Egypt, that is, by those who are not God's "Chosen People." Paul knows that this sort of debate is not the first time it

---

[4] Campbell, *The Deliverance of God*, 777.

has come up in Israelite history. A nearly identical discussion took place during the days of the prophets Isaiah and Jeremiah. Isaiah prophesied that God would use the idolatrous King Cyrus to accomplish His will. When many Israelites were indignant that God might raise up a foreign ruler to carry out His will, Isaiah reminded them that God was like a potter who could make whatever He wanted from clay (Isa 54:9). A similar discussion took place during the days of Jeremiah. In Jeremiah 18, we read that God is like a potter who can make whatever He wants from a lump of clay. It is to these sorts of historical discussions that Paul refers in Romans 9:21-24.

Western theology has committed a terrible disservice to this imagery of a potter and clay by making it seem as if God is a deterministic puppet master up in heaven pulling the strings of people and nations down here on earth. This is exactly the opposite of what Isaiah, Jeremiah, and Paul meant by using this terminology. In Jeremiah 18, for example, while God is equated with the potter, God calls upon Israel to turn from her wicked ways and obey His voice so that they, as the pot which God is fashioning, will not be marred (cf. Jer 18:8-11). God calls upon Israel to come into conformity to the work of His hands. If they do not, they will become marred, and He will have to reform the clay again into another vessel (Jer 18:4). He does not destroy or discard the clay; He simply forms it into another pot which will be used for a different purpose. A similar understanding is seen in Isaiah 54 and Romans 9.

There is no deterministic message in the image of the potter and the clay in Isaiah 54, Jeremiah 18, or Romans 9. If we accept the deterministic perspective of these texts, just imagine for a

moment what sort of God is being portrayed. H. H. Rowley sums
it up best:

> Neither Jeremiah nor Paul had in mind an aimless dilettante, work-
> ing in a casual and haphazard way, turning out vessels according to
> the chance whim of the moment ... To suppose that a crazy potter,
> who made vessels with no other thought than that he would after-
> wards knock them to pieces, is the type and figure of God, is su-
> premely dishonoring to God. The vessel of dishonor which the pot-
> ter makes is still something that he wants, and that has a definite
> use ... The instruments of wrath ... were what the New Testament
> calls 'vessels of dishonor,' serving God indeed, but with no exalted
> service. They were not puppets in His hand, compelled to do His
> will without moral responsibility for their deed, but chosen because
> He saw that the very iniquity of their heart would lead them to the
> course that He could use.[5]

Neither Isaiah, nor Jeremiah, nor Paul had in mind a potter
who purposefully created pots just so that He could smash them.
No potter would do that, then or now. Instead, God is the wise
potter who works with the clay to form useful tools. The vessels
of "dishonor" are not vessels which are destroyed, but vessels
which will be used in "ignoble" ways. They still serve important
purposes and help with vital tasks, but they are not vessels of
honor. Typically, vessels of dishonor do end up being destroyed
(which is not necessarily hell!), but this is not because the potter
made them for such a purpose, but because unclean vessels, when

---

[5] H. H. Rowley, *The Biblical Doctrine of Election* (London: Lutterworth,
1953), 40-41, 128.

they have served their purpose, are usually not useful for anything else.

And what makes one vessel clean or unclean? As H. H. Rowley pointed out above, God allows humans to determine what kind of vessel they will be, and then He uses those who have made themselves vessels of dishonor. A careful reading of Romans 9:22 reveals this very point. W. E. Vine, in his *Expository Dictionary of New Testament Words*, says that the word "destruction" is used "metaphorically of men persistent in evil (Rom 9:22), where 'fitted' is in the middle voice, indicating that the vessels of wrath fitted themselves for destruction."[6]

Again, none of this has anything to do with whether or not a person goes to heaven or hell after death. The way a vessel is used refers primarily to how God uses individuals, kings, and nations *in this life*. Marston and Forster add this:

> The basic lump that forms a nation will either be built up or broken down by the Lord, *depending on their own moral response*. If a nation does repent and God builds them up, then it is for him alone to decide how the finished vessel will fit into his plan ... God alone determines the special features / privileges / responsibilities of a particular nation.[7]

Paul goes on to say in Romans 9:21 that if God wants to take one lump of clay (one nation) and give part of it an honorable

---

[6] W. E. Vine, Merrill F. Unger, and William White Jr., *Vine's Complete Expository Dictionary of Old and New Testament Words* (Nashville: Thomas Nelson, 1985), 2:165.

[7] Forster and Marston, *God's Strategy*, 74.

task and the other part a dishonorable task, He can do that if He wants—*which is exactly what He has done with Israel.* Faithful Israel continues to be used by God to advance the Kingdom and spread the gospel (which Paul himself exemplifies, Rom 11:1), while unfaithful Israel is used by God to bring reconciliation to the rest of the world (Rom 11:15). This reveals that even "dishonorable" tasks are not demeaning or shameful. God obviously would receive even more glory if all Israel had remained faithful to Him, and through their faithfulness, had introduced reconciliation to the world. But this did not happen. Israel's failure, however, did not mean that God's plan had failed. No, God continued to provide purpose and usefulness to the "vessels of dishonor," so that they accomplished His will in other ways. This is the *true* sovereignty of God, which is Paul's point.

In Paul's mind, the sovereignty of God is more closely related to the wisdom and love of God than to His power and control. God does not muscle His way through time, forcing people to do His will despite their desires or wishes. No, God has given people a significant degree of freedom, and in order for this freedom to be truly free, God Himself honors this gift of freedom. However, this does not mean that God's hands are tied. God, in His infinite wisdom, is able to shift and adjust to the rebellious ways of mankind so that when vessels which God has prepared for honor end up in dishonorable situations, God is still able to accomplish His plans and purposes through their lives, albeit in a different way than originally intended. He does so in a loving and gracious way, even with the vessels of dishonor.

This reveals that when it comes to vessels of honor or dishonor, it is not the vessels themselves who are honored or dishonored, but God Himself. When God uses a vessel of dishonor, He is using a vessel for His own purposes, even though *that vessel had dishonored Him* through disobedience, hard-heartedness, or outright rebellion. This is what happened with Pharaoh and with Israel.

> Israel is known to be God's special people, entrusted with his oracles, etc. (Rom 3:2; 9:4-5). When people see the repentant section of Israel, living in harmony with God's will and exhibiting the fruits of his Spirit (Gal 5:22-23), it will be just like looking at a beautiful gold vase. Glory and honor will then be brought to the master of the house. When, however, anyone looks at that section of God's people who are living in rebellion against him, then no-honor is likely to be given to God. Perhaps even the name of God may be blasphemed among the Gentiles because of them (Rom 2:24).[8]

When this idea of the potter and the clay is properly understood, a beautiful picture of God emerges. God desires that all people come to Him, live in faithfulness to Him, and seek to serve Him in this world. When this happens, He is honored, and is able to easily invite such people to participate with Him in His work in this world. When, however, people and nations do not follow God or live in faithfulness to Him, He is dishonored by such behavior. But far from destroying such "vessels of dishonor," He is still able to work with them to accomplish His purposes. He does not want the dishonorable vessels to end up destroying themselves, but wants to reveal His power to them and the consequences of their decisions (which Paul calls wrath), and so He endures their dishonor with patience and much longsuffering

---

[8] Ibid., 75.

(Rom 9:22).

This line of argument is further supported by the statements of Paul in Romans 9:22-23. In Romans 9:22 Paul raises the question about how God deals with the vessels of wrath prepared for destruction. It is important to note that the word "His" in *His* wrath of Romans 9:22 is not found in the Greek. God does not want to show *His* wrath to the vessels of dishonor, but rather, to show them *the* wrath and destruction to which they are headed *if* they continue on the path they are traveling. God wants to warn them about the coming wrath; He is not threatening to send it. When read this way, God's power is in contrast to wrath; not in concert with it. He wants to unveil the source of wrath (sin and human rebellion) and the consequences of wrath (death and destruction), but show that His power of grace, mercy, and forgiveness defeats even wrath.

And how does God reveal His power and deal with the vessels of wrath which are headed for destruction? Not with anger or hate, but with longsuffering. He does not destroy them, but seeks to deliver them. Romans 9:23 begins with a Greek *hina* clause which shows purpose or intent. God is longsuffering toward the vessels of dishonor *in order that* "He might make known the riches of His glory on the vessels of mercy."

From Romans 9:23 then, it appears that Paul may actually be arguing that God bears with much longsuffering the vessels of dishonor headed for destruction *so that* they might become vessels of honor. Remember, if the honor and dishonor is directed toward God, then the vessels which are dishonoring God can become vessels which bring honor to Him *only* if He bears with them in longsuffering and does not immediately destroy them. A person which dishonors God may become a person which honors God if he or she recognizes God's patience with them and power in holding back the wrath that should have fallen upon them when they sinned (cf. Rom 5:12-21; 2 Cor 5:19).

This then helps clarify Paul's statement in Romans 9:24, where he refers to both Jews and Gentiles as being among those whom God has called. As a result of the honorable Jewish people becoming dishonorable, the dishonorable Gentiles had now become honorable, so that there were honorable vessels among both Jews and Gentiles. And as for those who were still dishonorable, Paul goes on in Romans 9:25–11:36 to discuss how God is patient and longsuffering toward them as well so that they too might be "saved."

With all this in mind, then, we could read Romans 9:22-24 as follows:

> *What if God, wanting to reveal wrath for what it is and make His power known, endured with much longsuffering the vessels of dishonor which were headed for destruction, so that He might make known the riches of His glory upon vessels of honor—which is the plan He has prepared beforehand for glory—and He did this not only for the Jews, but also for the Gentiles?*

Read this way, God does not want to show the vessels of mercy how wonderful He is by creating and destroying vessels of wrath, but instead seeks to show His mercy to those under wrath by enduring their rebellion patiently in the hopes that they would see His mercy *and become* vessels of honor. This has been God's plan to glorify Himself since the beginning!

That this is what Paul means is seen by looking at his statement in Romans 11:32: "For God has committed them all to disobedience, that He might have mercy on all." God is longsuffering toward those who are in rebellion so that He can display His grace and mercy to them, and in so doing, the vessels headed for destruction might instead become vessels headed for glory.

God does not create two classes of people, one to destroy and one to bless. No, all people are under sin and wrath, living as vessels of dishonor. But God is patient and longsuffering, wanting to make known to all the riches of His mercy so that all might become vessels of honor. In this way, He seeks for the vessels of dishonor to become vessels of honor, just as happened with the Gentiles (Rom 9:25-26), and can happen to Israel again (Rom 9:33). Though a veil is over Israel's hearts, it will be taken away if they truly seek God (2 Cor 3:14-4:6). "A vessel of wrath could turn to the Lord and thus become a vessel of mercy, upon whom God would show his glory."[9]

This way of reading the text makes so much more sense. Imagine a man who wants to show his wife how much he loves her and how good he is to her. Would he do this by going next door and beating up his neighbor's wife before coming home and saying, "See how good I am to you? I don't beat you up like I did her." What would you think of such a person? Or imagine a father with two children who sought to show his love for one by torturing the second. What kind of father is this? Yet this is the sort of God that Reformed theology presents to the world. By saying that God creates some people just so He can demonstrate

[9] Ibid., 76.

His wrath upon them and in so doing demonstrate His love and mercy to those who don't get His wrath, is to present a sadistic and cruel deity that is not worthy of anyone's worship.

It is much better to see God as a God who loves all and works with all to bring all into the experience of His love. Though there are people who are headed for destruction (this doesn't mean hell!), God is patient with them, seeking to show them the kindness of His mercy so that they might become people headed for honorable service in His Kingdom. This has been God's glorious plan since the beginning, and this is what He is working out with the Jews and also with the Gentiles.

CONCLUSION

Though a full understanding of Romans 9:10-24 would require a detailed analysis of Romans 9–11, which in turn demands a full study of Paul's entire letter to the Romans, this brief study has hopefully provided a glimpse at how Paul's ideas in Romans 9–11 about election fit with the rest of what the Bible teaches on this topic. Paul believes that election can be both corporate and individual, and that election is not to eternal life, but to service in this life. Paul illustrates this teaching on election by pointing to the individuals Jacob and Esau, and the nations that came from them, Israel and Edom, and how God used both for His purposes and will. Paul also uses the illustration of the hardening of Pharaoh's heart, and how even Pharaoh's proud rebellion was useful for God to glorify Himself and reveal His power to Israel and Egypt. This led Paul to conclude that God can use both Jews and Gentiles for His ongoing purpose to bless, reconcile, and redeem the world.

Hopefully, this sort of understanding of Romans 9:10-24 still passes the litmus test of Romans 9:14. What test is that? One objection that Calvinists sometimes have to the Arminian understanding of Romans 9–11 is that the Arminian understanding rarely raises the objection in Romans 9:14 that God appears to be unjust. Calvinists say that "The question of injustice in God never arises in the Arminian theory. For according to the Arminian, God is not arbitrary in His election, since He foresees who will be good or bad, or who will have faith."[1] This is a valid point. When Paul is properly understood, the question of injustice must arise. Just as the question about whether or not we can sin all we want is a litmus test for whether or not we have properly taught grace (Rom 6:1), so also, the question about God's justice is a litmus test for whether or not we have properly taught election. The explanation of Romans 9:10-24 presented above does pass this litmus test.

We have seen that God chose people and nations to serve in different ways for His redemptive purposes in the world. This raises questions about *why* God chooses one person or one nation to serve in one way, and another person or nation to serve in another. Furthermore, it seems unfair or unjust that one person or nation is called by God to seemingly accomplish more in His plan for world history than some other person or nation. For example, why did God raise up Paul to carry the message of the gospel of Jesus Christ to the Gentiles rather than some other person? For that matter, why didn't God raise up ten Pauls, or a hundred, or a thousand? Why doesn't God raise up you or me to be a modern-day Paul? The answer to these questions is that we simply do not know. It may seem unfair, unjust, or unwise, but it is not. God

---

[1] Edwin H. Palmer, *The Five Points of Calvinism*, Enl. ed. (Grand Rapids: Baker, 1980), 33.

chose Jacob over Esau, Israel over Edom, and some Gentiles over the Jews, all as part of His plan to bring redemption to the entire world. Does this seem unjust? Yes.

But we must not go so far into the apparent injustice of God as our Calvinistic friends by saying that God chooses whom He will bless with everlasting life, and whom He will damn to everlasting destruction. While this sort of idea also raises the objection of injustice with God, this is because this sort of idea *truly* is unjust. Just because a particular reading of Romans 9 raises the objection of injustice with God, this does not mean that that particular reading of Romans 9 is correct.

To conclude then, the point of Romans 9–11 is not about some strange act of God whereby He chooses some to receive eternal life while others get damned to hell by God's sovereign eternal decree. No, the point of Romans 9–11 is that God sought to bless the entire world by raising up Israel to be a light and a blessing to others, but Israel failed in this task. Israel's failure, however, did not mean the failure of God's plan. God, in His wisdom and resourcefulness, was able to bring Gentiles to Himself even through Israel's failure.

> When the elect nation stumbles and falls, God puts aside the elect and then does the unthinkable. He elects the non-elect, that is, the Gentiles.[2]

Why does God do this? According to Paul, so that the Gentiles

[2] Robert D. Brinsmead, "Election in the Light of the Old Testament Background," *Present Truth Magazine* (Vol 45), 12.

may now be a blessing to the Jews! This is Paul's point in Romans 11:13-24. Israel, the elect nation, became non-elect through her disobedience, and in so doing, the non-elect Gentiles became elect. Note that none of this has anything whatsoever to do with people's eternal destinies. Paul is not talking about whether or not people can lose their eternal life. Instead, he is talking about positions of service in God's plan for the world. God wants to bless the world, and while He chose Israel for this purpose, He now seeks to do it through the Gentiles, until ultimately all will be blessed by God (Rev 21:23-26; 22:2).

This understanding fits perfectly with Paul's overall theme in Romans about the gospel as the power of God unto salvation for all believers. Salvation is not about believing in Jesus for eternal life (though that is a central part of the gospel), but is also about living with purpose and significance as members of the New Creation in this life. This is Paul's message in Romans, and chapters 9–11 fit perfectly into this overall theme.

This study of Romans 9:10-24 began with a brief summary of why Paul embarked on this discussion of election in the first place. The reason is because near the end of Romans 8, Paul had written that God's purposes for His people will never fail. The obvious objection to this was that God's purposes for Israel had apparently failed, and so how could members of Christ's church know that God's purposes for us will not also fail? Romans 9 contains the beginning of that answer. Paul's initial answer is that God, in His infinite wisdom, is still able to accomplish His purposes in and through us, even when *we* fail. As Paul writes elsewhere, "if we are faithless, He remains faithful" (2 Tim 2:13).

Paul goes on to point out in the rest of chapter 9 and on into

Romans 10–11 that even though Israel failed in her calling, mission, and purpose, God grafted in the Gentiles so that she might succeed in her calling, mission, and purpose. In an amazing display of God's resourcefulness, Paul says that "if their being cast away is the reconciliation of the world, what will their acceptance be but life from the dead?" (Rom 11:15). God is not done with Israel. He has not cast Israel aside. He has not forsaken or abandoned her. Quite to the contrary, though they have turned away from God, God is able to use even their rebellion to accomplish reconciliation for the world, so that they might be given over to jealousy, and return to God (Rom 11:11) until "of Him and through Him and to Him are all things, to whom be glory forever. Amen" (Rom 11:36).

Paul's point from Romans 8 stands. Nothing can separate us from the love God. What God has started, He will bring to completion. This is the truth that spurs the believer on toward faithful living, which Paul describes in Romans 12–15. Romans 9–11 is not a self-contained excursus which has little to do with the rest of Paul's letter, but is central to everything Paul has written, and is a critical step to getting from the theology of Romans 1–8 to the practical Christian living of Romans 12–15. God has chosen us for service, and even if we mess up, God's purposes for us will not be deterred. So don't live in fear of mistakes, but step out in faith to present yourself to God as holy, accepted, and ready for service (Rom 12:1-2).

ABOUT JEREMY MYERS

Jeremy Myers is an author, blogger, podcaster, and Bible teacher. Much of his content can be found at RedeemingGod.com, where he seeks to help liberate people from the shackles of religion. He lives in Oregon with his wife and three beautiful daughters.

If you appreciated the content of this book, would you consider recommending it to your friends and leaving a review on Amazon? Thanks!

JOIN JEREMY MYERS AND LEARN MORE

Take Bible and theology courses by joining Jeremy at
RedeemingGod.com/join/

Receive updates about free books, discounted books,
and new books by joining Jeremy at
RedeemingGod.com/read-books/

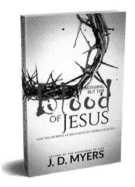

NOTHING BUT THE BLOOD OF JESUS: HOW THE SACRIFICE OF JESUS SAVES THE WORLD FROM SIN

Do you have difficulties reconciling God's behavior in the Old Testament with that of Jesus in the New?

Do you find yourself trying to rationalize God's violent demeanor in the Bible to unbelievers or even to yourself?

Does it seem disconcerting that God tells us not to kill others but He then takes part in some of the bloodiest wars and vindictive genocides in history?

The answer to all such questions is found in Jesus on the cross. By focusing your eyes on Jesus Christ and Him crucified, you come to understand that God was never angry at human sinners, and that no blood sacrifice was ever needed to purchase God's love, forgiveness, grace, and mercy.

In *Nothing but the Blood of Jesus*, J. D. Myers shows how the death of Jesus on the cross reveals the truth about the five concepts of sin, law, sacrifice, scapegoating, and bloodshed. After carefully defining each, this book shows how these definitions provide clarity on numerous biblical texts.

Building on his previous book, 'The Atonement of God', the work of René Girard and a solid grounding in the Scriptures, Jeremy Myers shares fresh and challenging insights with us about sin, law, sacrifice, scapegoating and blood. This book reveals to us how truly precious the blood of Jesus is and the way of escaping the cycle of blame, rivalry, scapegoating, sacrifice and violence that has plagued humanity since the time of Cain and Abel. 'Nothing but the Blood of Jesus' is an important and timely literary contribution to a world desperately in need of the non-violent message of Jesus. –Wesley Rostoll

So grateful to able to read such a profound insight into the Bible, and the truths it reveals, in this new book by Jeremy Myers. When reading both this book and the Atonement of God, I couldn't help but feel like the two disciples that walked with Jesus after His resurrection, scripture says that their eyes were opened…they knew Him… and they said to one another, 'Did not our heart burn within us while He talked with us on the road, and while He opened the Scriptures to us?'

My heart was so filled with joy while reading this book. Jeremy you've reminded me once more that as you walk with Jesus and spend time in His presence, He talks to you and reveals Himself through the Scriptures. –Amazon Reader

Purchase the eBook for $8.99
Purchase the Paperback for $14.99

THE ATONEMENT OF GOD: BUILDING YOUR THEOLOGY ON A CRUCIVISION OF GOD

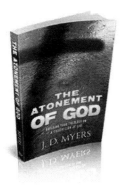

After reading this book, you will never read the Bible the same way again.

By reading this book, you will learn to see God in a whole new light. You will also learn to see yourself in a whole new light, and learn to live life in a whole new way.

The book begins with a short explanation of the various views of the atonement, including an explanation and defense of the "Non-Violent View" of the atonement. This view argues that God did not need or demand the death of Jesus in order to forgive sins. In fact, God has never been angry with us at all, but has always loved and always forgiven.

Following this explanation of the atonement, J. D. Myers takes you on a journey through 10 areas of theology which are radically changed and transformed by the Non-Violent view of the atonement. Read this book, and let your life and theology look more and more like Jesus Christ!

REVIEWS FROM AMAZON

Outstanding book! Thank you for helping me understand "Crucivision" and the "Non-Violent Atonement." Together, they help it all make sense and fit so well into my personal thinking about God. I am encouraged to be truly free to love and forgive, because God has always loved and forgiven without condition, because Christ exemplified this grace on the Cross, and because the Holy Spirit is in the midst of all life, continuing to show the way through people like you. –Samuel R. Mayer

If you have the same resolve as Paul, to know nothing but Jesus and Him crucified (2 Cor 2:2), then this book is for you. I read it the first time from start to finish on Father's Day ... no coincidence. This book revealed Father God's true character; not as an angry wrathful God, but as a kind loving merciful Father to us. Share in Jeremy's revelation concerning Jesus' crucifixion, and how this "vision" of the crucifixion (hence "crucivision") will make you fall in love with Jesus all over again, in a new and deeper way than you could imagine. Buy a copy for a friend—you won't want to give up your copy because you will want to read it again and again until the Holy Spirit makes Jeremy's revelation your revelation. –Amy

This book gives another view of the doctrines we have been taught all of our lives. And this actually makes more sense than what we have heard. I myself have had some of these thoughts but couldn't quite make the sense of it all by myself. J.D. Myers helped me answer some questions and settle some confusion for my doctrinal views. This is truly a refreshing read. Jesus really is the demonstration of who God is and God is much easier to understand than being so mean and vindictive in the Old Testament. The tension between the wrath of God and His justice and the love of God are eased when reading this understanding of the atonement. Read with an open mind and enjoy! –Clare Brownlee

Purchase the eBook for $4.99
Purchase the Paperback for $11.99

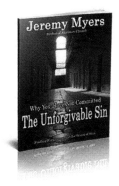

WHY YOU HAVE NOT COMMITTED THE UNFORGIVABLE SIN: FINDING FORGIVENESS FOR THE WORST OF SINS

Are you afraid that you have committed the unforgivable sin?

In this book, you will learn what this sin is and why you have not committed it. After surveying the various views about blasphemy against the Holy Spirit and examining Matthew 12:31-32, you will learn what the sin is and how it is committed.

As a result of reading this book, you will gain freedom from the fear of committing the worst of all sins, and learn how much God loves you!

REVIEWS FROM AMAZON

This book addressed things I have struggled and felt pandered to for years, and helped to bring wholeness to my heart again. –Natalie Fleming

A great read, on a controversial subject; biblical, historical and contextually treated to give the greatest understanding. May be the best on this subject (and there is very few) ever written. – Tony Vance

You must read this book. Forgiveness is necessary to see your blessings. So if you purchase this book, [you will have] no regrets. –Virtuous Woman

Jeremy Myers covers this most difficult topic thoroughly and with great compassion. –J. Holland

Good study. Very helpful. A must read. I like this study because it was an in depth study of the scripture. –Rose Knowles

Excellent read and helpful the reader offers hope for all who may be effected by this subject. He includes e-mails from people, [and] is very thorough. –Richie

Wonderful explication of the unpardonable sin. God loves you more than you know. May Jesus Christ be with you always. –Robert M Sawin III

Excellent book! Highly recommend for anyone who has anxiety and fear about having committed the unforgivable sin. –William Tom

As someone who is constantly worried that they have disappointed or offended God, this book was, quite literally, a "Godsend." I thought I had committed this sin as I swore against the Holy Spirit in my mind. It only started after reading the verse about it in the Bible. The swear words against Him came into my mind over and over and I couldn't seem to stop no matter how much I prayed. I was convinced I was going to hell and cried constantly. I was extremely worried and depressed. This book has allowed me to breathe again, to have hope again. Thank you, Jeremy. I will read and re-read. I believe this book was definitely God inspired. I only wish I had found it sooner. –Sue

Purchase the eBook for $5.99
Purchase the Paperback for $5.99

SKELETON CHURCH: A BARE-BONES DEFINITION OF CHURCH (PREFACE TO THE CLOSE YOUR CHURCH FOR GOOD BOOK SERIES)

The church has a skeleton which is identical in all types of churches. Unity and peace can develop in Christianity if we recognize this skeleton as the simple, bare-bones definition of church. But when we focus on the outer trappings—the skin, hair, and eye color, the clothes, the muscle tone, and other outward appearances—division and strife form within the church.

Let us return to the skeleton church and grow in unity once again.

REVIEWS FROM AMAZON

My church gathering is struggling to break away from traditions which keep us from following Jesus into the world. Jeremy's book lends encouragement and helpful information to groups like us. –Robert A. White

I worried about buying another book that aimed at reducing things to a simple minimum, but the associations of the author along with the price gave me reason to hope and means to see. I really liked this book. First, because it wasn't identical to what other simple church people are saying. He adds unique elements that are worth reading. Second, the size is small enough to read, think, and pray about without getting lost. –Abel Barba

In *Skeleton Church*, Jeremy Myers makes us rethink church. For Myers, the church isn't a style of worship, a row of pews, or even a building. Instead, the church is the people of God, which provides the basic skeletal structure of the church. The muscles, parts, and flesh of the church are how we carry Jesus' mission into our own neighborhoods in our own unique ways. This eBook will make you see the church differently. –Travis Mamone

This book gets back to the basics of the New Testament church— who we are as Christians and what our perspective should be in the world we live in today. Jeremy cuts away all the institutional layers of a church and gets to the heart of our purpose as Christians in the world we live in and how to affect the people around us with God heart and view in mind. Not a physical church in mind. It was a great book and I have read it twice now. –Vaughn Bender

The Skeleton Church ... Oh. My. Word. Why aren't more people reading this!? It was well-written, explained everything beautifully, and it was one of the best explanations of how God intended for church to be. Not to mention an easy read! The author took it all apart, the church, and showed us how it should be. He made it real. If you are searching to find something or someone to show you what God intended for the church, this is the book you need to read. –Ericka

Purchase the Paperback for $5.99
Purchase the eBook for $2.99

THE DEATH AND RESURRECTION OF THE CHURCH (VOLUME 1 IN THE CLOSE YOUR CHURCH FOR GOOD BOOK SERIES)

In a day when many are looking for ways to revitalize the church, Jeremy Myers argues that the church should die.

This is not only because of the universal principle that death precedes resurrection, but also because the church has adopted certain Satanic values and goals and the only way to break free from our enslavement to these values is to die.

But death will not be the end of the church, just as death was not the end of Jesus. If the church follows Jesus into death, and even to the hellish places on earth, it is only then that the church will rise again to new life and vibrancy in the Kingdom of God.

REVIEWS FROM AMAZON

I have often thought on the church and how its acceptance of corporate methods and assimilation of cultural media mores taints its mission but Jeremy Myers eloquently captures in words the true crux of the matter—that the church is not a social club for do-gooders but to disseminate the good news to all the nooks and crannies in the world and particularly and primarily those bastions in the reign of evil. That the "gates of Hell" Jesus pronounces indicate that the church is in an offensive, not defensive, posture as gates are defensive structures.

I must confess that in reading I was inclined to be in agreement as many of the same thinkers that Myers riffs upon have influenced me also—Walter Wink, Robert Farrar Capon, Greg Boyd, NT Wright, etc. So as I read, I frequently nodded my head in agreement. –GN Trifanaff

The book is well written, easy to understand, organized and consistent thoughts. It rightfully makes the reader at least think about things as … is "the way we have always done it" necessarily the Biblical or Christ-like way, or is it in fact very sinful?! I would recommend the book for pastors and church officers; those who have the most moving-and-shaking clout to implement changes, or keep things the same. –Joel M. Wilson

Absolutely phenomenal. Unless we let go of everything Adamic in our nature, we cannot embrace anything Christlike. For the church to die, we the individual temples must dig our graves. It is a must read for all who take issues about the body of Christ seriously. –Mordecai Petersburg

Purchase the eBook for $6.99
Purchase the Paperback for $8.99

PUT SERVICE BACK INTO THE CHURCH SERVICE (VOLUME 2 IN THE CLOSE YOUR CHURCH FOR GOOD BOOK SERIES)

Churches around the world are trying to revitalize their church services. There is almost nothing they will not try. Some embark on multi-million dollar building campaigns while others sell their buildings to plant home churches. Some hire celebrity pastors to attract crowds of people, while others hire no clergy so that there can be open sharing in the service.

Yet despite everything churches have tried, few focus much time, money, or energy on the one thing that churches are supposed to be doing: loving and serving others like Jesus.

Put Service Back into the Church Service challenges readers to follow a few simple principles and put a few ideas into practice which will help churches of all types and sizes make serving others the primary emphasis of a church service.

REVIEWS FROM AMAZON

Jeremy challenges church addicts, those addicted to an unending parade of church buildings, church services, Bible studies, church programs and more to follow Jesus into our communities, communities filled with lonely, hurting people and BE the church, loving the people in our world with the love of Jesus. Do we need another training program, another seminar, another church building, a remodeled church building, more staff, updated music, or does our world need us, the followers of Jesus, to BE the church in the world? The book is well-written, challenging and a book that really can make a difference not only in our churches, but also and especially in our neighborhoods and communities. —Charles Epworth

Do you ever have an unexplained frustration with your church, its service or programs? Do you ever feel like you are "spinning your wheels" when it comes to reaching others for Christ? This book helps to explain why this might be happening, and presents a convincing argument for why today's church services are mostly ineffective and inefficient. You will read concepts explained that you've not fully heard before. And you will get hints as to how it could, or should, work. —MikeM

I just finished *Put Service Back Into Church Service* by Jeremy Myers, and as with his others books I have read on the church, it was very challenging. For those who love Jesus, but are questioning the function of the traditional brick and mortar church, and their role in it, this is a must read. It may be a bit unsettling to the reader who is still entrenched in traditional "church," but it will make you think, and possibly re-evaluate your role in the church. Get this book, and all others on the church by Jeremy. —Ward Kelly

Purchase the eBook for $5.99
Purchase the Paperback for $5.99

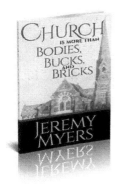

CHURCH IS MORE THAN BODIES, BUCKS, & BRICKS (VOLUME 3 IN THE CLOSE YOUR CHURCH FOR GOOD BOOK SERIES)

Many people define church as a place and time where people gather, a way for ministry money to be given and spent, and a building in which people regularly meet on Sunday mornings.

In this book, author and blogger Jeremy Myers shows that church is more than bodies, bucks, and bricks.

Church is the people of God who follow Jesus into the world, and we can be the church no matter how many people we are with, no matter the size of our church budget, and regardless of whether we have a church building or not.

By abandoning our emphasis on more people, bigger budgets, and newer buildings, we may actually liberate the church to better follow Jesus into the world.

REVIEWS FROM AMAZON

This book does more than just identify issues that have been bothering me about church as we know it, but it goes into history and explains how we got here. In this way it is similar to Viola's *Pagan Christianity*, but I found it a much more enjoyable read. Jeremy goes into more detail on the three issues he covers as well as giving a lot of practical advice on how to remedy these situations. –Portent

This book surprised me. I have never read anything from this author previously. The chapters on the evolution of the tithe were eye openers. This is something that has bothered me for years in the ministry. It may be truth that is too expensive to believe when it comes to feeding the monster. –Karl Ingersoll

Since I returned from Africa 20 years ago I have struggled with going to church back in the States. This book helped me not feel guilty and has helped me process this struggle. It is challenging and overflows with practical suggestions. He loves the church despite its imperfections and suggests ways to break the bondage we find ourselves in. –Truealian

Jeremy Meyers always writes a challenging book ... It seems the American church (as a whole) is very comfortable with the way things are ... The challenge is to get out of the brick and mortar buildings and stagnant programs and minister to the needy in person with funds in hand to meet their needs especially to the widows and orphans as we are directed in the scriptures. –GGTexas

Purchase the eBook for $7.99
Purchase the Paperback for $9.99

DYING TO RELIGION AND EMPIRE (VOLUME 4 IN THE CLOSE YOUR CHURCH FOR GOOD BOOK SERIES)

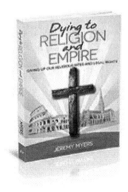

Could Christianity exist without religious rites or legal rights? In *Dying to Religion and Empire*, I not only answer this question with an emphatic "Yes!" but argue that if the church is going to thrive in the coming decades, we must give up our religious rites and legal rights.

Regarding religious rites, I call upon the church to abandon the quasi-magical traditions of water baptism and the Lord's Supper and transform or redeem these practices so that they reflect the symbolic meaning and intent which they had in New Testament times.

Furthermore, the church has become far too dependent upon certain legal rights for our continued existence. Ideas such as the right to life, liberty, and the pursuit of happiness are not conducive to living as the people of God who are called to follow Jesus into servanthood and death. Also, reliance upon the freedom of speech, the freedom of assembly, and other such freedoms as established by the Bill of Rights have made the church a servant of the state rather than a servant of God and the gospel. Such freedoms must be forsaken if we are going to live within the rule and reign of God on earth.

This book not only challenges religious and political liberals but conservatives as well. It is a call to leave behind the comfortable religion we know, and follow Jesus into the uncertain and wild ways of radical discipleship. To rise and live in the reality of God's Kingdom, we must first die to religion and empire.

REVIEWS FROM AMAZON

Jeremy is one of the freshest, freest authors out there— and you need to hear what he has to say. This book is startling and new in thought and conclusion. Are the "sacraments" inviolate? Why? Do you worship at a secular altar? Conservative? Liberal? Be prepared to open your eyes. Mr. Myers will not let you keep sleeping!

For all free-thinkers, for all who consider themselves "spiritual," for all who have come out or are on the way out of "Babylon," this is a new book for you! Treat yourself, buy this book and enjoy it! –Shawn P. Smith

Jeremy Myers is one or the most thought provoking authors that I read, this book has really helped me to look outside the box and start thinking how can I make more sense of my relationship with Christ and how can I show others in a way that impacts them the way that Jesus' disciples impacted their world. Great book, great author. –Brett Hotchkiss

Purchase the eBook for $6.99
Purchase the Paperback for $9.99

CRUCIFORM PASTORAL LEADERSHIP (VOLUME 5 IN THE CLOSE YOUR CHURCH FOR GOOD BOOK SERIES)

This book is forthcoming in early 2017.

The final volume in the *Close Your Church for Good* book series look at issues related to pastoral leadership in the church. It discusses topics such as preaching and pastoral pay from the perspective of the cross.

The best way pastors can lead their church is by following Jesus to the cross!

This book will be published in early 2017.

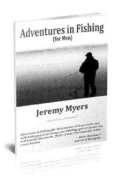

ADVENTURES IN FISHING (FOR MEN)

Adventures in Fishing (for Men) is a satirical look at evangelism and church growth strategies.

Using fictional accounts from his attempts to become a world-famous fisherman, Jeremy Myers shows how many of the evangelism and church growth strategies of today do little to actually reach the world for Jesus Christ.

Adventures in Fishing (for Men) pokes fun at some of the popular evangelistic techniques and strategies endorsed and practiced by many Christians in today's churches. The stories in this book show in humorous detail how little we understand the culture that surrounds us or how to properly reach people with the gospel of Jesus Christ. The story also shows how much time, energy, and money goes into evangelism preparation and training with the end result being that churches rarely accomplish any actual evangelism.

REVIEWS FROM AMAZON

I found *Adventures in Fishing (For Men)* quite funny! Jeremy Myers does a great job shining the light on some of the more common practices in Evangelism today. His allegory gently points to the foolishness that is found within a system that takes the preaching of the gospel and tries to reduce it to a simplified formula. A formula that takes what should be an organic, Spirit led experience and turns it into a gospel that is nutritionally benign.

If you have ever EE'd someone you may find Myers' book offensive, but if you have come to the place where you realize that Evangelism isn't a matter of a script and checklists, then you might benefit from this light-hearted peek at Evangelism today. –Jennifer L. Davis

Adventures in Fishing (for Men) is good book in understanding evangelism to be more than just being a set of methods or to do list to follow. –Ashok Daniel

Purchase the eBook for $0.99

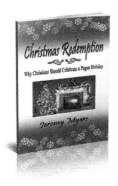

CHRISTMAS REDEMPTION: WHY CHRISTIANS SHOULD CELEBRATE A PAGAN HOLIDAY

Christmas Redemption looks at some of the symbolism and traditions of Christmas, including gifts, the Christmas tree, and even Santa Claus and shows how all of these can be celebrated and enjoyed by Christians as a true and accurate reflection of the gospel.

Though Christmas used to be a pagan holiday, it has been redeemed by Jesus.

If you have been told that Christmas is a pagan holiday and is based on the Roman festival of Saturnalia, or if you have been told that putting up a Christmas tree is idolatrous, or if you have been told that Santa Claus is Satanic and teaches children to be greedy, then you must read this book! In it, you will learn that all of these Christmas traditions have been redeemed by Jesus and are good and healthy ways of celebrating the truth of the gospel and the grace of Jesus Christ.

REVIEWS FROM AMAZON

Too many times we as Christians want to condemn nearly everything around us and in so doing become much like the Pharisees and religious leaders that Jesus encountered. I recommend this book to everyone who has concerns of how and why we celebrate

Christmas. I recommend it to those who do not have any qualms in celebrating but may not know the history of Christmas. I recommend this book to everyone, no matter who or where you are, no matter your background or beliefs, no matter whether you are young or old. –David H.

Very informative book dealing with the roots of our modern Christmas traditions. The Biblical teaching on redemption is excellent! Highly recommended. –Tamara

Finally, an educated writing about Christmas traditions. I have every book Jeremy Myers has written. His writings are fresh and truthful. –Retlaw "Steadfast"

This is a wonderful book full of hope and joy. The book explains where Christmas traditions originated and how they have been changed and been adapted over the years. The hope that the grace that is hidden in the celebrations will turn more hearts to the Lord's call is very evident. Jeremy Myers has given us a lovely gift this Christmas. His insights will lift our hearts and remain with us a long time. –Janet Cardoza

I love how the author uses multiple sources to back up his opinions. He doesn't just use bible verses, he goes back into the history of the topics (pagan rituals, Santa, etc.) as well. Great book! –Jenna G.

<u>Purchase the eBook</u> for $2.99

BOOK PUBLISHING INSTRUCTIONS: A STEP-BY-STEP GUIDE TO PUBLISHING YOUR BOOK AS A PAPERBACK AND EBOOK

The dirty little secret of the publishing industry is that authors don't really need publishing companies any longer. If you want to get published, you can!

This book gives you everything you need to take your unfinished manuscript and get it into print and into the hands of readers. It shows you how to format your manuscript for printing as a paperback and preparing the files for digital eReaders like the Kindle, iPad, and Nook.

This book provides tips and suggestions for editing and typesetting your book, inserting interior images, designing a book cover, and even marketing your book so that people will buy it and read it. Detailed descriptions of what to do are accompanied by screenshots for each step. Additional tools, tips, and websites are also provided which will help get your book published.

If you have a book idea, you need to read this book.

REVIEWS FROM AMAZON

I self-published my first book with the "assistance" of a publishing company. In the end I was extremely unhappy for various reasons

... Jeremy Myers' book ... does not try to impress with all kinds of "learned quotations" but gets right to the thrust of things, plain and simple. For me this book will be a constant companion as I work on a considerable list of books on Christian doctrines. Whether you are a new aspiring author or one with a book or so behind you, save yourself much effort and frustration by investing in this book.
–Gerrie Malan

This book was incredibly helpful. I am in the process of writing my first book and the info in here has really helped me go into this process with a plan. I now realize how incredibly naive I was about what goes into publishing a book, yet instead of feeling over-whelmed, I now feel prepared for the task. Jeremy has laid out the steps to every aspect of publishing step by step as though they were recipes in a cook book. From writing with Styles and using the Style guide to incorporating images and page layouts, it is all there and will end up saving you hours of time in the editing phase.
–W. Rostoll

Purchase the eBook for $9.99
Purchase the Paperback for $14.99

THE LIE — A SHORT STORY

When one billion people disappear from earth, what explanation does the president provide? Is he telling the truth, or exposing an age-old lie?

This fictional short story contains his televised speech.

Have you ever wondered what the antichrist will say when a billion people disappear from planet earth at the rapture? Here is a fictional account of what he might say.

Purchase the eBook for $0.99

JOIN JEREMY MYERS AND LEARN MORE

Take Bible and theology courses by joining Jeremy at
RedeemingGod.com/join/

Receive updates about free books, discounted books, and new books by joining Jeremy at
RedeemingGod.com/read-books/

Printed in Great Britain
by Amazon